209923

The Age of Conformity

ALAN Chester VALENTINE

The
Age of Conformity

HENRY REGNERY COMPANY, *Chicago*
1954

To
James Sibley Watson
1860–1951

Preface

A BOOK that is critical of one's own society is not easy to write or likely to be popular. We Americans may be interested in seeing ourselves as others see us, but if the vision is unflattering and yet probably true, we dislike to face the facts. I share some of the resentment others may feel against the author of this book.

But after considerable experience in education and government, and some perspective on business, I believe there are things which should be said about America and that it is not unpatriotic to say them. Since some of them are painful, I find consolation in the fact that the ideas and opinions offered here have all been previously expressed by others. I have merely tried to synthesize them.

Every page owes something to earlier writers. It is therefore impossible to offer full acknowledgments, but where a special debt has been incurred an attempt has been made to record it. If through ignorance or inadvertence someone has been done an injustice I am sorry.

A. V.

Acknowledgments

The author records his appreciation to the following in connection with quotations in this book:

To Rosemary Benét and Brandt and Brandt, from *Nightmare at Noon* by Stephen Vincent Benét; to Harcourt, Brace and Co., from *Introduction to Social Ethics* by John M. Mechlin and from *Two Cheers for Democracy* by E. M. Forster; to Charles Scribner and Sons, from *Character and Opinion in the United States* by George Santayana; to The Bobbs Merrill Company, from *Company Manners* by Louis Kronenberger; to The Macmillan Company, from *The Degradation of Democratic Dogma* by Henry and Brooks Adams and from *The Dynasts,* by Thomas Hardy; to W. W. Norton and Company, from *The Revolt of the Masses* by José Ortega y Gasset; to the Yale University Press, from *The American Mind* by Henry Steele Commager; to Harper and Brothers, from *Crowd Culture* by Bernard Iddings Bell and from an article in Harper's Magazine by Thornton Wilder; to The Viking Press, from *Acton's Political Philosophy* by G. E. Fasnacht, quoting Lord Acton; to Houghton Mifflin and Company, from *The Education of Henry Adams* by Henry Adams; to The University of Oklahoma Press, from *From a Front Row Seat* by Nicholas Roosevelt; and to Henry Holt and Company and Longmans, Green and Company for joint permission to print an unidentified quotation from William James.

Also special appreciation for personal permission to quote them, to Associate Justice of the Supreme Court Robert H. Jackson, Secretary of State John Foster Dulles, President Harold Dodds of Princeton, Dean George Packer Berry of the Harvard Medical School, Judge Learned Hand and Walter Lippmann; also to Mrs. Alfred North Whitehead for permission to quote from her husband.

A. V.

Contents

The Age of Conformity

1

Dilemmas of Democracy

There are certain words,
Our own and others' we're used to—words we've used,
Heard, had to recite, forgotten. . . .
Liberty, equality, fraternity.
To none will we sell, refuse or deny right or justice.
We hold these truths to be self-evident.

I am merely saying—what if these words pass?
What if they pass and are gone and are no more,
Eviscerated, blotted out of the world?
　　　—STEPHEN VINCENT BENÉT, *Nightmare at Noon.*

MANY AMERICANS have given their lives to keep words like liberty from being blotted out of the world, and more Americans will do so. We preserve the words; the danger is that we will let them be cheapened by our own carelessness or distorted by demagogues, until they lose the heart of their meaning. We have seen what mockery dictators can make of words like truth and democracy, but we have not recognized that through our own confusions we ourselves can debase them in less obvious ways.

This is not the first age of great crisis, but it is the first whose remedies depend not on a few people but on a hundred million, and the first where the nature of the crisis is so little understood by the many who must meet it. We must face unpleasant facts about ourselves and yet refuse to be cynical or despairing.

1

Many Americans are troubled that our concepts of democracy are being watered down by the undemanding standards of our popular culture. One man is disturbed by our mounting juvenile delinquency, another by our commonplace culture, a third by our fuzzy thinking, a fourth by our political amorality. Few have tried to analyze the relations between these phenomena or to consider their over-all connection with developments like urbanization, industrial complexity, big government and popular sovereignty. These factors need synthesis. Aware of the tremendous difficulties involved, I attempt that synthesis, and hope that it will challenge others to dig deeper.

Such an attempt can produce, at this early stage, little more than half the truth. No one can tell the whole truth about democracy because no one knows or could know it. Democracy is nations, forces, habits, emotions and promises. To try to evaluate all its aspects, even in a single country like America, would require infinite self-confidence and infinite words. One can begin so overwhelming an assignment only by selecting some point of approach and limiting oneself to material relevant to it. One must resist the temptation to supply concrete examples to support generalizations which would make the material more topical but less detached. Though that is the only way, it is an unsatisfactory way, for a man can see in democracy whatever he looks for, and emerge with conclusions that fortify his preconceptions. The honest man must try to resist that deeply satisfying experience.

The selected point of approach is whether increasing popular sovereignty brings a decline in political and cultural values. The pursuit of this idea requires more emphasis on the faults of our democracy than on its virtues. This imbalance can be criticized as incomplete or pessimistic, but a diagnosis need not be complete in order to be valid. A medical man consulted about overeating or anemia does not feel that he must offer the patient assurances that his muscular tone is satisfactory or his brain normal. If one who believes in the great promise of democracy concludes that it is failing to realize that promise, he must risk offending his fellow-citizens by suggesting that they are overindulging themselves.

Three trends are apparent throughout the western world. The economic trend is toward a highly industrialized and urbanized society. The political trend is toward direct and centralized popular government, in which the numerical plurality is increasingly dominant. The social trend is toward the acceptance of popular standards of cultural quality. Each of these trends bears cause and effect relationships to the others. The growth of industry and large cities has affected democratic politics and culture. The increased political power and assertiveness of what used to be called the common man has influenced the procedures and culture of democracy and altered its economic balance. National culture in turn determines political and economic policies. It seems clear that politics, economics and culture must therefore move in unison if democracy is to realize its promise of fostering human excellence. Since politics and economics are expressions and vehicles of society, the crucial issue is the quality of its culture.

A complete study would include a more thorough investigation of other democracies than is attempted here. But it is in the United States that the combined development of industrialization, popular sovereignty and mass culture has reached its most impressive proportions. America is the outstanding example of powerful mechanized democracy and its fate will determine the fate of the free world. Other democratic nations are alternately hopeful that American freedom will continue to flourish and expand, and fearful that their own cultures will become too like that of America.

Inevitably the standards of America become the center of this study, but a European reader may find they provide interesting parallels with his own.

Europeans are reluctant, and with reason, to imitate too closely the American way of life. They have observed, for example, that disrespect for law is mounting in America, and accepted by Americans with perplexed passivity. In a public address on November 2, 1953, Supreme Court Justice Robert H. Jackson said that the United States is "plagued with unprecedented juvenile delinquency, gangsterism and shocking crimes followed by long-delayed punishment, or none. . . . Our people, appalled by the magnitude and stubbornness of the manifestations of lawlessness, tend to sink into a suicidal fatalism that accepts violence, crime, injustice and misgovernment as part of the natural and changeless order of things."

Though America's delinquency, after the manner of things American, may be the biggest and best, Western Europeans who read of it with a pleased sense of superior virtue are living in glass houses. In their own countries there are evidences of similar trends. The London *Times* is not given to public exposure of British faults, but in a leading editorial in August, 1953, it discussed reports of a "fairly typical cross-section of the community" in which forty per cent of the young people studied had been "officially delinquent" at some stage of their lives, while as many more had been "unofficially delinquent." Though the *Times* did not confirm the percentages as necessarily typical of all British youth, it agreed that ethical weaknesses are general and mounting in British society, and continued:

"The attitude reported by Mr. Mays is similar to that which leads youngsters to scrounge materials, with no sense of wrong-doing, to slash seats in cinemas, to steal usable electric bulbs from trains, or to smash windows on unfinished

4

housing estates. . . . The evidence of similar adult dishonesty, although fragmentary, is impressive. . . . Travelling without paying the proper fare, like pilfering from book shops, seems to be as prevalent among the middle classes as among the masses. Pilfering at the workshop or the office seems to be common. The building worker and the electrician who do private jobs for private householders in their spare time, with materials stolen from firms, are well-known types."

Lest a British reader infer that his country is singled out for unhappy association with American social customs, he is hastily assured that reports from the Continent indicate similar declines in ethical standards. Many of the examples may seem trivial and their discussion alarmist, but when cumulated they go far beyond normal ethical misadventures and reveal a problem that permeates free society.

At this point the defense rises to protest that these are typical postwar phenomena and only temporary; and that although democratic societies may not yet have achieved new heights of cultural excellence or ethics, they have raised their general levels, and that upon this new plateau higher peaks of spiritual and moral quality will ultimately be erected. But has the qualitative general level of democratic culture really been raised, or only the level of material standards and literacy? Does that limited kind of improvement ensure later eminences of human excellence? So heavy an emphasis on material and technical values may deter rather than encourage the exaltation of cultural intangibles.

What is the reason why the spirits of free men are not more uplifted by their freedom? They seem more acquiescent than enthusiastic, more energetic than creative. Even their gaiety seems a little artificial—not the spontaneous zest and *élan* of a happy and confident people. Probably no society in history has been more marked by spiritual enervation and the psychoses of frustration than the very society that won freedom in order to pursue happiness. Only in its conquests of the natural elements does it display an adventurous spirit; in art, letters and life there is more emphasis on perplexity and futility than on beauty or exaltation. Perhaps it could not be otherwise in a world threatened by destruction, but it has been in such times of fear and danger that earlier generations sought consolation in the values of the spirit. One cannot escape the conclusion that the causes go deeper than recent wars and atomic bombs, for even before those holocausts the sources of men's inspiration seemed to be running dry.

Perhaps the explanation lies in the fact that the current generation is the victim of the concurrent crumbling of several pillars on which civilization was built: faith in a personal God and in organized religion; faith in the perfectability of man and the certainty of progress; faith in fixed absolutes to guide thought and action. Men have largely discarded the compass of spiritual direction and the charts of moral absolutes. Science has not been really reconciled with religion, or the new forces of industrialism with traditional social and economic mores. The barbarism that men of the nineteenth century thought they had vanquished forever has returned to challenge civilization itself by belittling the dignity of the individual.

Lacking compelling religious convictions, confused and inundated by materialism and an undemanding scientific impersonality, millions of men and women in Europe accepted to some degree the philosophy and ends of which Hitler and Stalin were the extreme exponents. Many citizens of the western hemisphere have not entirely escaped the infections of the anti-humanist power-worship of the dictators. We lack the spiritual cohesion that held society together, and even the leaders of the free world sometimes

6

seem like small boys whistling through the dark to keep their courage up.

To meet the challenges of the new barbarism, the free world has offered little except force against force—except immediate palliations for immediate crises, vague humanitarianism, and the hope that a benevolent super-state could be created that would somehow prove more wise and virtuous than its citizens. As we observe how free men like ourselves will abandon personal responsibility and will delegate their salvation to other men called governments, we can understand better how Germans came to accept Hitler. Democracy moves toward total government in the names of efficiency and social welfare, yet total government leaves men diminished, for when they accept it they renounce part of their own mental and moral stature.

When men feel confused or belittled they retreat into the primitive and create new idols to replace the ones that seem to have failed them. This is what modern man is doing without knowing that he is retreating or that his actions express the primitive. For the graven images of earlier times he is substituting test tubes, production lines, the majority and the state. Yet history shows that whatever men build without a spiritual end ultimately recoils upon them with annihilating force. To retire from the battlefield of moral responsibility, to seek new idols more primitive in their forms of force than the previous ones, is no way to win or hold freedom. Men still resist outward tyranny, but no longer in the spirit of Jefferson's conviction that resistance to tyranny is obedience to God.

Democratic man thus finds himself fumbling amid dilemmas. Is democracy a political system or an all-pervasive social philosophy? Does it lead inevitably to equalitarianism and if so can equalitarianism satisfy human instincts and ideals? Can a large, urbanized, industrialized society function successfully as a total democracy under political institutions designed to serve a smaller, rural society with a different concept of democratic government? Must popular sovereignty ultimately result in absolutism by a majority, enforced through its use of strong social pressures upon individuals to conform? Are popular tastes and elevated culture mutually exclusive?

There are more than two horns to these dilemmas, but the basic issues are whether democracy shall seek quantity or quality as its cultural goal, and materialism or humanism as its working method. The people are deciding these issues, often unconsciously. There is no retreat from their decisions, once finally made. The stakes rest on the vision and understanding of the average American. There is little evidence that he understands the gravity of the issue or that he is objective about it. The case for democracy as a way of life seems to him, rightly, so superior to the case for the totalitarianism of Hitler or Stalin that he does not visualize the dangers of its spiritual decline. Human freedom started on the right track upward; it is the obligation of its present beneficiaries to see that it stays there. To do so they must analyze those aspects of our new mass political and cultural sovereignty that are impeding the fulfillment of the democratic dream. In its effort to do so, this book makes no attempt to conceal personal judgments. Its writer begs his readers not to ignore the problems even if they disagree with his inferences, but to consider the issues and draw their own conclusions. The choices of free men should be made with open eyes. If Americans want all the pleasures of materialism and full equality, they will have to pay for them in the deterioration of their freedom and culture. The choices they make—perhaps the choices they have already made— will determine whether the great promises that inspired democracy will be fulfilled.

2

The Framework of Freedom

*I agree with you that there is a natural aristocracy
among men. The grounds of this are virtue and talents. . . . [This] natural aristocracy I consider the
most precious gift of nature, for the instruction, the
trusts, the government of society. . . . May we not
even say, that that form of government is the best that
provides the most effectively for a pure selection of
these natural* aristoi *into the offices of government?*
—THOMAS JEFFERSON *to John Adams.*

DEMOCRACY has become a state of mind. It is man's
optimism about man. Based on faith, hope and parity,
it assumes that society is perfectible, that men are reasonable
and that equality is desirable. It is a compound of Christian
ideals and philosophical Utopias, infused with eighteenth-
century reason, nineteenth-century humanitarianism and
twentieth-century materialism.

The original concept of democracy was less all-inclusive.
For centuries it was only a political ideal; not until nearly
1700 was it embodied in political machinery. Only after it
had become firmly established in America did it begin to
transcend the theoretical and the political and become an
emotional attitude permeating all society's thought and functions.

Scholarship assigns to the Greeks the first significant thinking leading to the democratic state. Upon that foundation

9

political philosophers and statesmen over the centuries added their accretions, while countless other men, less remembered by history, painfully advanced by trial and error the practice of free government. Free men of today owe their freedom to those earlier pilots and spade-workers of democracy, as well as to the founders of the American republic. Those founders wanted first of all a government that would endure. They were not willing to risk its durability by attempting too much of the theoretical perfection of pure democracy. They did not even want democracy as the word is understood today; the idea would have alarmed them. To them and their fellows the word democracy was generally a term of disrespect, allied to anarchy and mob rule. The Constitution these men hammered out was a compromise between the liberal ideal of self-government and the conservative tradition of an aristocrat-led stability.

In their political discussions they distinguished between the people and the state. This distinction was an outgrowth of English constitutional development, where the objective of the people was to limit the power of the king but not to usurp his administrative function. America had disposed of its king and thereby created a political vacuum; the Convention was faced with the unique task of filling that vacuum with an entirely new government. Carrying the British experience to its logical conclusion, they did not intend to establish a government in which the people were directly substituted for a king. Though the people were to be the ultimate sovereigns, they were not to assume the administrative functions of government, or even to guide its affairs too intimately. When they wrote that the new government derived its "just powers from the *consent* of the governed" they meant consent, not initiative; they meant that the popular power should be confirmatory rather than directive.

To them the problem was how to enable the people to control government without operating it; how to organize the power of a free populace but, as Madison put it, to "refine" their will. They sought to bring to disorganized American society an order and a leadership which would protect the citizen from the tyranny of a transient majority of his fellows as well as the tyranny of his officers of government. By such devices as the division of powers, the establishment of representative government and the limitation of federal government authority in relation to the separate states, they believed they had provided a solution. The founders instinctively agreed with Burke that popular government is not simply a matter of arithmetic; on important issues they wanted the will of the people to be a considered and filtered judgment rather than a temporary mathematical plurality.

They went further, and attempted to bring into popular government something of the historical awareness that they themselves possessed, and that in legal history has been called the spirit of the common law. The will of the people was to be, in the words of Burke "a partnership not only between those who are living, but between those who are living, those who are dead, and those who are to be born." This envisaged a political system that would represent all facets of popular wisdom: tradition, unwritten laws and new ideas. The individual would serve in his separate capacities as local citizen, state citizen and national citizen, tempering his reactions in each capacity with remembrance of things past and hopes of things to come. This attitude, the founders thought, would not only make free government safe for the people but safe from the people's selfishness and volatility. The new republic was consequently democratic in the sense that ultimate power lay with the people, but it was not total popular sovereignty because it adopted devices to keep the people from using their power too directly or arbitrarily, or in disregard of experience. The judgment and property of the outvoted was carefully protected from the wishes of the numerically superior. As a partnership with those who are dead and those yet to be born, it was meant to be an alliance with traditional culture. Instead of discarding the past, the founders of the republic moored their ship of state to it.

To them the problem was political and the solution was political. They had little time to speculate together (though some speculated separately) upon how the new government would affect the economic and cultural life of its future citizens. They had to leave such things to time and their successors, and this made the political machinery they set up seem in one way unrealistic: it operated in a kind of splendid isolation from the daily lives and pursuits of its citizens. It was almost as though the founders thought that on election days the voter would march to the ballot box and record his share of the people's mandate, insulated by reason and patriotism from all the mundane influences and emotions that on all the other days of the year largely determined his actions. The Jeffersons and Madisons had less chance than we to observe how greatly a man's political judgment is an end product of the prejudices, self-seekings and conditionings to which, in so forceful a society, he is inevitably exposed.

Certainly even the most prescient of eighteenth-century minds could not have foreseen how the development of mechanized democratic government would make politics and culture part of the same mass operation. Communication and propaganda have become so easy and effective, standardization and conformity so great, statesmen so quickly responsive to public opinion, that the will of the majority, often casually and irresponsibly expressed, diminishes the prestige of the ballot until half the voting population does not go to the polls in national elections. Modern democratic government could become so responsive to this informal sovereignty of popular expression that the decisions of election days would be only post-mortems. Had men like Jefferson and Hamilton been able to guess the pressures which a dominant majority would come to exert, in ways quite outside political machinery, they would have felt even more strongly the need for the kind of citizen education that would produce and then support leadership of the highest quality.

Increasing popular sovereignty and its results have therefore pointed up the fact that the quality of democratic government depends upon the mental maturity and standards of the average voter. This is a matter on which Jefferson was eloquent. As "the Father of American Democracy" he is often pictured as the great exponent of the direct rule of the people, with unqualified belief in their capacity to govern wisely. That concept is not derived from Jefferson's own words, for his confidence in democracy was clearly and repeatedly qualified.

It is true that Jefferson had an almost mystical belief in the good character and moral wisdom of the American farmer. He sometimes expressed this in large terms, as in his letter of August 10, 1787, to Peter Carr:

"State a moral case to a plowman and a professor. The former will decide it as well, and often better than the latter, because he has not been led astray by artificial rules."

Read hurriedly, these words seem to indicate a firm faith in the political wisdom of the common man. But they are interesting for what they avoid saying. Jefferson does not state that the plowman could decide the average political question better than the professor, or indeed any question requiring knowledge, or a trained mind, or humane culture or reasoned judgment. He limits the superior or equal judgment of the plowman to a "moral case," by which he seems to mean some specific issue of ethical judgment. He does not suggest that the plowman could decide that issue, or any other, more wisely than a philosopher like Franklin, a doctor like Benjamin Rush, or a landed aristocrat like Jefferson himself. He makes his case only against a man whose training lets him be "led astray by artificial rules." Presumably he meant the kind of pedant that can always be found in scholarship, law or government. He would hardly have advocated a general system of education and a national university had he taken so dim a view of all professors.

Often and emphatically Jefferson makes it clear that "no republic can maintain itself in strength" without "general education . . . to enable every man to judge for himself what will secure or endanger his freedom," as he wrote Governor Tyler on May 26, 1810. This need for education was always a stated or implied codicil to Jefferson's faith in the people as their own rulers. As early as 1782 he wrote in his *Notes on Virginia:*

". . . every government degenerates when trusted to the rulers of the people alone. The people themselves, therefore, are the only safe depositories. And to render even them safe, their minds must be improved to a certain degree."

And universal education to that specific end was a condition to Jefferson's faith in free government.

In 1786 he wrote to George Wythe:

"I think by far the most important bill in our whole code is that for the diffusion of knowledge among the people. No other sure foundation can be devised for the preservation of peace and happiness. . . . Preach a crusade against ignorance; establish and improve the law for educating the common people . . . the people alone can protect us against the evils (of misgovernment)."

He meant the kind of education that would provide value judgments as well as vocational skills.

The citizens whom Jefferson thought of as capable (with the help of education) of self-government were landowning agriculturalists. He hoped that they would always comprise the majority of Americans. Himself a product of eighteenth-century thought, he saw American farmers in the somewhat romantic terms of Goldsmith's

> . . . *bold peasantry, its country's pride,*
> *Which once destroyed can never be supplied.*

—an elevated concept of the agricultural society he knew in his own Virginia; men with a farm-ownership stake in the stability of the new republic, independent and uncorrupted by the life of industry and great cities, inheriting a traditional respect for law and order. His enfranchised bold peasantry did not of course include black slaves, women, or the later millions of immigrants from countries without such traditions. He took it for granted that the racial constitution, social mores, political ideals and religious concepts of future Americans would be like those of the men he knew.

And who were they? They were derived from the British Isles, with a few from Holland, Ireland, Germany, France and Scandinavia. Most of them had inherited the traditions of the Magna Carta, local self-government and individual initiative. Many were nonconformists in religion, with all that nonconformity meant in independence and stern morality. Only if the republic were dominated by such men did Jefferson have faith in society's capacity for full self-government. Like Hamilton he feared the masses, though he feared them differently. To Jefferson the masses were large industrial populations huddled in great cities, and the great danger to the republic was the development of a factory society with its unstable urban populations. "The mobs of great cities," he wrote in his *Notes on Virginia,* "add just so much to the support of pure government as sores do to the strength

15

of the human body." And to Madison on December 20, 1787:

"I think our governments will remain virtuous for many centuries; as long as they are chiefly agricultural; and this will be as long as there shall be vacant lands in any part of America. When they get piled upon one another in large cities, as in Europe, they will become corrupt, as in Europe."

Nor did Jefferson's faith in the common man lead him to advocate the elimination of a governing class. He believed the new republic must be led by an aristocracy of talents and virtues, recruited from all classes of society and nurtured by the educational system he proposed. It is ironic that the nation has never come again as close to Jefferson's *aristoi* as in his own time, and that its closest nineteenth-century approximation was the English governing class he had defied.

Hamilton's ideas about democracy and education were not so dissimilar as sometimes reported. He too believed a system of national education essential to republican government, though he may have been less hopeful of the results. He drafted the 1787 report which created the University of the State of New York, and drew up the recommendation which Washington presented to Congress in his address advocating a national university.

Even more than Jefferson, Hamilton feared that the will of the people would be volatile and emotional if officers of government deferred too completely to popular ideas. "On the whole," he wrote to Colonel Edward Carrington in 1792, "the only enemy which republicanism has to fear in this country is the spirit of faction and anarchy . . . and the demagogues who have produced the disorder will use it for their own aggrandisement."

"The republican principle," he wrote in *The Federalist*, "does not require an unqualified complaisance to every sudden breeze of passion, or to every transient impulse which the people may receive from the arts of men, who flatter their prejudices and betray their interests. . . . The people commonly *intend* the *public good* . . . but their good sense would despise the adulator who should pretend they always *reason right* about the *means* of promoting it."

The essential difference between Jefferson and Hamilton was with regard to the motives of free men. Jefferson believed that most citizens of the new republic would put the common interest before their own, and that their reason would guide them more than their emotions. Hamilton and Madison were less optimistic; they feared that most men would put their personal interests first, but hoped that by the compromise or canceling out of special interests the welfare of all would reach reasonable balance. It was the latter point of view which strongly urged the checks and balances in the Constitution; it was the recrudescence of the Jeffersonian faith that has worked to modify them. The difference of opinion endures to confuse democratic government.

A few other early citizens sensed the ultimate inseparability of culture and politics as democracy developed, and were concerned lest either pull the other down. Shortly after 1776 some of them began to draft comprehensive plans to elevate national culture. Franklin organized and encouraged philosophy as well as scientific knowledge; Dr. Benjamin Rush published his *Thoughts upon the Mode of Education Proper in a Republic*. A few years later the American Philosophical Society offered a prize for "the best system of liberal education and literary instruction adapted to the genius of the United States, comprehending also a plan for instituting and conducting public schools in this country, on principles of the most extensive utility." Noah Webster presented large projects for the education of youth "in a manner appropriate to American society and government." Washington, John Adams, Madison, and later John Quincy Adams, also thought and wrote on national education.

What was and was not accomplished by these efforts is a matter of history. If their original intent had been meticulously followed, American government might have seemed better or worse to its present citizens, but its tone would have been more elevated. The strains on democratic government through rapid social and economic changes required political adaptations to meet them, but they might have been kept more in line with the original concepts. The nation has spent immense sums on universal education, but its aims have been deflected from the purposes of the founding fathers, and its results do not seem to have elevated government or society to a point where reason and restraint rule.

In adapting the original republic to its modern needs, liberals of today have urged that the cure for the ills of democracy is more democracy, but full popular sovereignty has created more problems than it has solved. They have advocated a more powerful and centralized state, but that has not brought a more unified society. Reversing their earlier roles, liberals now exalt centralized government while conservatives try to reduce it, and this has left both groups confused between their traditions and their current practice. Meanwhile the people as a whole, disregarding the earlier distinction between themselves and their government, have taken over the functions (though not the manners) of the kingly role. This leaves modern courtiers with nothing to court but majority opinion, and the people no one to admire except themselves. Few Americans realize how far their society and their government have departed from the ideals and intentions of its founders. While we praise their ideals from our platforms, we obscure them in our practices.

3

Democracy Breaks Out

The duties of any public office are so simple or admit of being made so simple that any man can in a short time be master of them.—ANDREW JACKSON.

Uniformity never met with more favor than in a revolution raised in the name of the rights and liberties of men.—BENJAMIN CONSTANT *on the French Revolution.*

WHEN the Convention drew up the Constitution," wrote Lord Acton, ". . . every effort was made, and every scheme was invented, to curb inevitable democracy." The election of Andrew Jackson to the presidency rejected the spirit of those curbs. It was the first great political victory of the common man and a clear omen that full popular sovereignty was on the way. It turned the nation's course from the original concept of a republic toward the total democracy it has become. In that election the pioneers of the new West and the artisans of the East asserted their numerical superiority over the more established and cultivated citizens, and declared their intention to govern. The common man found the experience a heady one; he has repeated it whenever possible and with increasing confidence. The changes in government and culture which resulted have set the tone of modern America, and for that reason the age of Jackson will be used here as a symbol of the popular revolt from the traditions and leadership of upper-class society. Ortega might have called it the revolt of the masses.

19

It is doubtful that any nation can start down the road of popular sovereignty without going all the way. Had Andrew Jackson never won an election the victory of the common man would have been only postponed, for forces were developing to make it inevitable. Modern industry brought economic bargaining power to the working man, and political influence was sure to follow. It would be absurd to give the impression that the Jacksonian revolution was sudden and complete; or that it did not have its virtues as well as its dangers; or that it alone was responsible for the later trends toward popular rule. But it did move the nation, in theory and practice, from a republic carefully constructed to ensure mature leadership toward a popular democracy that offered no affirmative plan to produce political quality. It demolished earlier cultural patterns and left a vacuum which mediocrity rushed to fill. Had American popular sovereignty developed more slowly or under less iconoclastic direction it might have produced a more mature and cultivated society.

The Jackson regime had no deep concern with the minds or morals of the people. Some of its spokesmen denied that it was a function of government to encourage the development of science, education, literature or the arts, which they derided as effeminate if not undemocratic. The coonskin caps, tobacco juice and bootmarks they brought and left on the furniture of the White House were symbolic of their intention to tread heavily on the traditions and standards of their predecessors. The spirit of the revolt was more temperate than that of the French Revolution, but it sought equality through the same methods—the belittling of the superior in cultivation and manners.

To these new ruling servants of the people the art of government was an easy affair which earlier statesmen, to serve their own purposes, had pretended was difficult. Jackson would not have agreed with Lord Bryce that "some problems are beyond the competence of the average man . . . when a question of intricacy presents itself, requiring either keen insight, exact reasoning, or wide knowledge, [the average man] is at fault." Since to the Jacksonians the art of government was so simple, it obviously did not need the aid of education, and they neglected to forward the plans of their predecessors to elevate the electorate.

The belief that the common man is competent, without further education, to administer the state left its imprint on American thought. Thousands of platform speakers have assured the average citizen of his full political competence, and he has acted accordingly. Though many Americans did not accept as a reasoned philosophy the belief that "any man can in a short time be master of" the duties of public office, society accepted the spirit of that credo and abandoned any idea of an aristocracy of virtue and talents. Since Jackson's election no great political leader has looked all around education, plumbed its depths, considered its quality in relation to the quality of American society, or (like Washington, Jefferson and John Quincy Adams) consistently urged its promotion as a cultural force. They have paid eloquent tributes to education; they have urged some segment of it; they have voted large sums for its support. But none of them emphasized it as a qualitative and ethical necessity to the elevation of free government, and nailed their political flag to that mast. Nor did the great leaders of private affairs devote their best talents and energies to the cultural quality of the nation. They generously gave millions for private endowments for some single institution or some special aspect of education, but none of them gave their most encompassing and penetrating thought to the national significance of their foundations or to the over-all qualitative necessities of the nation in terms of education.

Without such leadership, public and private, to counter-act the public surge, the nation increasingly accepted political and cultural mediocrity. This led naturally to the identification of democracy with equalitarianism, for if the average man was qualified without preparation to rule, there was little reason to develop or exalt the superior, or even to recognize it. The results were soon noticed by foreign visitors like Mrs. Trollope, Harriet Martineau and Charles Dickens. Edward Dicey, for twenty years an editor of the London *Observer*, summarized their reactions when he wrote in 1863: "The very circumstances that make the United States unat-tractive as a residence for the man of wealth and refinement are a positive boon to those who possess neither of these attributes." And Lord Bryce wrote thirty years later of American "insensibility to the nobler aspects and finer re-sponsibilities of national life," and of a "certain commonness of mind and tone, a want of dignity and elevation about the conduct of public affairs."

Especially since World War I the national trend has been away from appreciation of the exceptional toward concen-tration on the average, away from individual excellence toward the improvement of society *en masse*. The word *republic* has almost vanished from the national vocabulary and its actual meaning from the national mind; to recall it is to risk being branded a reactionary. The New Deal and the Fair Deal encouraged these attitudes. They settled the issue of democracy *versus* republic once and for all, and permanently established popular unlimited sovereignty as the goal. The only question still undecided is whether direct political rule by average men means cultural domination by average minds.

In purely political procedures the increase in popular sovereignty has made operation under the original Constitu-tion and Bill of Rights difficult. The governmental machinery established for the early republic was not intended for a nation with so highly centralized and all-pervasive a government so directly sensitive to the public will. Though the economic and political transformation has been gradual enough to permit the machinery of government to adjust itself and grind onward, that machinery as it is now operated does not serve efficiently a society so different in composition and outlook from that of 1790. The American federal government of today lurches along like an outdated vehicle loaded with too large a crew, being driven faster than it can safely go by a succession of drivers in disagreement about the road, and too deferential to inconsistent suggestions from the back seat. Proposals to reorganize the machinery are helpful, but they do not go deep enough to cope with changes so basic in American life and thought.

It is easy to see why the doctrine that the average man is by natural endowment competent to direct democracy has become so popular. It flatters the common man and gives him power; it makes few demands upon him for self-improvement, and leaves him free to pursue his personal ends. But when he accepted this pleasant assumption of his own effortless competence, the average citizen cut loose not only from the intention of the founding fathers but from the concepts that lay behind them. Those earlier philosophers of democracy did not conceive it as a political institution that could stand alone, independent of the ethics and culture of its citizens. To them, self-government was an integral part of a larger program for the general elevation of mankind, and inseparable from it. They conceived a social structure which would make men wise and moral, and therefore capable of self-government. They made the political freedom of man contingent upon the elevation of man, and proceeded to formulate a plan to that end. They would not have advocated a democracy whose citizens claimed the skill and power to

23

govern and yet took no serious steps that would qualify them to govern.

The deists and rationalists who speculated on democracy had a special reason for emphasizing that only men with trained reason and morality could operate a free government. They knew that in advancing their theories they had weakened those existing sanctions of civilization of which they had been critical. They knew that they must replace the old sanctions with new ones. They had attacked the dogmatisms of established religion and the anti-rationalism of the churches. Their substitute for religious dogma was a vague and flexible deism in which man was the center of the universe and the primary responsible character, with God relegated to remote supervision. Their substitute for the moral sanctions of the church was to have been the development of reason and morality in all men, and for that reason they sponsored the moral and general education that arose in their time. The words and actions of men like Franklin and Jefferson show how close they were to this rationalist doctrine.

Most Jacksonians and their successors in the capital were not familiar with these foundations and codicils of the democratic theory, or if familiar were impatient with such abstractions. To them the procedure of free government was far more simple. They used the political equality the democratic theory had given them to gain control of the machinery of government and to maintain it. They did not lack confidence in their capacity to operate it to their own satisfaction, without recourse to the troublesome pursuit of self-improvement or of the fancy and effete tags of upper-class cultivation. Under their competent but limited minds the nation flourished materially, but it did not develop the earlier plans to raise the standards of society. They neglected what the creators of self-government had believed essential to its success.

Had the concepts of the first presidents prevailed, there would now stand between the popular will and the actions of government a balance wheel of semi-permanent professional servants just below the cabinet level who, in ability, prestige and independence of political appointment and political pressures would stand in happy contrast with most present federal employees. Jackson's use of the spoils system destroyed the chance of that kind of a permanent undersecretariat of high excellence. Though civil service was later established as a substitute for it, civil service does not reach high enough in the hierarchy of government; it has emphasized tenure of office at a cost to quality of service; it does not attract men of the highest caliber, and it has become a union system for the protection of the employee rather than for the recruitment and elevation of high talent and devotion. Though civil service has modified the ills of the spoils system it has augmented the ills of mass time-serving. The quality of government has not improved with its expansion, and the ill-effects of its protection of mediocrity become more apparent with time.

The founders created an electoral college to temper and mature the will of the people by passing it through the judgment of the best minds of the nation, selected for that purpose. The members of that group were to meet and choose, without previous commitment or regard to party lines, the ablest man as president and the next ablest as vice-president. The growth of political parties, which choose rival slates of electors, with each elector pledged to vote for the party candidate, has nullified this device of the founders.

The original structure provided that though members of the House of Representatives should be elected by, and be directly responsible to, the people, senators were to represent the people only indirectly through the states and were to be chosen by the state legislatures. The direct election of senators has made the states less powerful and the Senate more directly responsive to the popular will. The Senate is no longer an effective restraining balance wheel upon popular sentiment. The original idea of the upper house has been so modified that many citizens in our larger states now favor reapportionment of senators on a straight population basis. Nor has the direct election of senators convincingly raised their average quality.

The initial safeguards against direct popular sovereignty have also been weakened by the referendum and recall, the direct election of some judges, the establishment of administrative law under the executive and outside the regular courts, the increasing deference of the judiciary to the climate of popular opinion, and the general decline of states rights.

In the long run the operation of the two-party system has probably made government more responsive to public opinion. Since party leaders are increasingly eager to please the voting majority, the party policies they adopt and the candidates they nominate are based primarily upon their capacity to win votes. Party bosses in smoke-filled rooms may once have flouted the popular will, but they no longer dare do so. Radio, television and the press now inform the average voter what is really going on at national conventions, and even the most powerful political boss knows that if he cannot guide public opinion he must defer to it. Especially when the deference of party leaders and even recent presidents to organized labor is considered, it seems clear that the direct power of the people over their government is all the greater because of the two-party system.

The executive, too, is increasingly sensitive to the reactions of the public. In recent years the White House has developed its own large staff to secure and interpret directly to the president the latest turns of popular sentiment. It also reverses the process by helping him to carry his thoughts directly to the people. Presidents sometimes send up trial balloons to get public reactions before a final decision. Through its vast departmental activities the executive branch of federal government is now in constant touch with farmers, labor leaders and business men, and this has increased the direct influence of the president on the people—and also the direct influence of the people on the president.

But more important than these changes in the formal and informal machinery of federal government are the new points of view in society. Some of these have been partly created by the expansion and penetration of government. The greater the power and participation of central government in the affairs of its citizens, the greater their tendency to depend on it for personal assistance. Many citizens who boast the American tradition of self-reliance and deplore the tendency to lean on government are quick to run to Washington for special favors for their businesses. Communities large and small almost automatically ask for federal aid in financing not only their local needs but their local ambitions. Pervasive government has also led private citizens into almost endless dealings with federal agencies. Favors, clarifications, interpretations, permits, renegotiations, price adjustments and contracts bring daily discussions between thousands of business men and federal officials all over the country as well as by trek to Washington. Price and wage controls, when existent, increase this communication by geometric ratios. The delays, uncertainties, irritations, time and expense involved do not add to the efficiency of either business or government, or increase mutual good will. Big government is not strengthening the self-reliance of Americans, and the situation gives point to Lord Acton's fear that socialism would prove "the infirmity that attends mature democracies."

Such developments add to the general confusion as to the place and functions of federal government in a democratic society. If Americans prefer total democracy with its concomitant big government, it is time they recognize the total losses, intangible as well as tangible, of that system, and ask themselves whether they are really willing to pay the bill. If they want that kind of government, then they must face up to the basic adjustments necessary to make it work better than at present.

The problems raised in this chapter are ones that develop through the mechanics of government, but improvements in political machinery are only part of the remedy. American ideals and mores are involved, and must also be considered. Politics is only the reflection of these, the mirror of a nation's culture.

4

Conflicts in Democracy

I had learned that in respect to political principle only the naive think they can be original. For the enduring principles are enduring because they reflect a very long experience.
            —WALTER LIPPMANN, The Good Society.

. . . of the deficiencies . . . which might seem to go deepest, are the prominence of inferior men in politics and the absence of distinguished figures.' . . . They are the fruits . . . of a theory which has confused equality of civil rights with equality of capacity.
            —JAMES BRYCE, The American Commonwealth.

THE EARLY statesmen of the American republic had two immediate fears—aggression from without and instability within. The nation they created has never been invaded and has survived civil war and drastic social change. Most Americans have been inclined to rest on that record of success, and not to trouble themselves about a third danger envisaged by the founders: that democracy might bring a mass domination that would level society downward from mediocrity to mediocrity until it became too mediocre to survive. They have not sought, as Hamilton did, for "a principle in government capable of resisting the popular current."

To prevent tyranny by government, the founders had provided the well-known checks and balances, and guaranteed powers to the states and specific rights to private citizens.

To prevent mass domination they also took steps, but these have not been equally stressed in most textbooks. By reserving to the states all powers not expressly granted to the federal government they set up barriers to protect that government from direct popular control. Lord Acton called this system "the one immortal tribute of America to political science, for state rights are at the same time the consummation and guard of democracy." The electoral college, the selection of senators by states, and the appointment rather than the direct election of judges were also measures to prevent "mobocracy." The rights of individuals and minorities were thought to be above alteration by popular majority alone, and those rights were also checks on the power of the majority as well as the power of government.

The trends of history have weakened acceptance of the original philosophy, and removed or circumvented the safeguards against direct popular sovereignty. A federal government of limited powers has become a centralized government of almost unrestricted authority. A national society once dominated by men of common race and tradition has become so variegated in racial origin, ideology, traditions and leadership that its only unities lie in a devotion to "democracy," security and material progress. Equality of political opportunity has been expanded in the direction of economic and social leveling.

The fact that a Constitution and a framework intended for one purpose has been inadequately adapted to another has increased the misunderstanding as to what democracy is and how it should operate. It is easy to say that democracy is the rule of the people, but that statement does not illumine political procedure. If it means that the people rule by pulling down, at stipulated intervals, the levers of voting machines, the definition is inadequate. If it means more than that, how much more?

Democracy is not difficult to define if it is considered solely in the historical and technical terms of the political scholar. To him, democracy is a system of government in which the electorate is able within the constitution to make, revise or unmake its government. But this definition is more academic than realistic. Democracy means far more than that to most of its citizens, and it is they who decide what democracy shall be. Phrases like "the democratic spirit," "the faith of democracy," and the familiar appellation "undemocratic" to almost anything unpalatable to the speaker (or almost anything qualitatively demanding), reveal that democracy has connotations far beyond the purely political. Many Americans insist that it means comfort and security for all as well as freedom for all.

If the average citizen should put on one side, for the moment, all that he expects from democracy, and try to define it only as an operating system, his concept of its operation would still be at some variance with the founders and the scholars. To him democracy means equal participation by all concerned in almost any kind of undertaking, with all decisions made after fair discussion by a numerical majority, and then accepted by the rest. The rights—and what is now equally important, the interests—of the minority, do not seem to concern him as much as they concerned the founders.

The trouble with that operating definition is that it does not make for real freedom of the individual, or for effective leadership by the most able, and it is not consistent with the careful logic upon which democratic government was built. It confuses majority rule with political freedom, and they are quite different matters.

In the eighteenth century they often seemed the same. That was because then the majority and the individual were both seeking freedom and both opposing the tyranny of kings and oligarchs. It was then in the interest of the majority to defend the individual against the common enemy of royal despotism; and it was in the interest of the ordinary individual to support majority rule, since it would give him a voice in government. In the twentieth century the partnership between majority rule and individual freedom is less logical, for their objectives are not necessarily common. The rule of kings has been replaced by the rule of the majority, which therefore tends to regard the rights and interests of the minority—the individual—as troublesome obstacles to the efficiency of its operations.

The word "minority" has even changed its connotations. It is ceasing to signify a group of men whose rights and interests, though temporarily outvoted, are essential to society and the functioning of government and therefore to be meticulously respected by the dominant majority. In the eyes of current pluralities, a minority is often no more than a regrettable impediment to action—a defeated group more to be pitied than respected, whose motives can be questioned or distorted for political purposes, and whose opinions are to be considered only when its votes are needed. Thinking along those lines could ultimately make a popular majority just as intolerant of any dissenting opinion as the worst tyrant—and more safely intolerant, since it has numbers on its side.

Hence the old conflict between liberty and repression does not end with the establishment of popular sovereignty but merely enters a new phase. In a closely-knit and powerful modern society, effective protection of minorities requires not only deference to the law but also to the spirit and traditions of free men. Adherence to them means refraining from the use of social pressures to bring conformity. That is the final test of the maturity of majority rule. Popular sovereignty means social freedom only if it curbs its insistence upon its own way, a fact which men in masses tend to ignore as their power increases.

It is true that the Constitution and the Bill of Rights still protect the citizen from specific political encroachments by his government, but they do not protect him from the decisions of the majority to make such encroachments legal, or from the extra-legal and non-political pressures of his fellow-citizens. As democracy becomes the rule of the simple majority it develops its own subtle forms of totalitarianism. Many American "liberals" argue that the state should re-organize society and improve the conditions of its citizens, whether they like it or not. Only the state, say these "liberals," is wise enough and strong enough to protect men against the oppression of dominant interest groups, and to organize the economy and social justice of the nation—and anything short of state action leaves democracy in the "horse and buggy era." These attitudes parallel what James Madison called "the old trick of turning every contingency into a resource for accumulating force in the government."

Under such theories the minority has no inalienable rights that the state may not abridge or suspend, with the claim that they impede the general interests of society. Even constitutional rights can be made subject to government interpretation and national emergency, and in recent decades the courts have shown a stronger tendency to support majority opinion or government policies; to adapt their interpretation of the existing law to the social climate around them. This makes personal freedom increasingly subject to popular verdicts that are sometimes only reflections of the transient emotional reactions of disparate groups, rather than the enduring purpose of a stable society.

"The state accepts the individual only in so far as his interests coincide with the state." What extreme liberal of the

33

Roosevelt regime said that? Those were the words of Mussolini in defining fascism.

It is not easy for a dominant majority to act with restraint when it feels itself in jeopardy or is disoriented by rapid social or economic change. Then emotions are high; then fear spreads its poisons and intolerance thrives and investigations become persecutions; then society attempts its own purification from subversives and forgets that the remedy can be more dangerous than the disease. At such times the conduct of the majority betrays how far it has lost its understanding of the true meaning of freedom.

The modern confusion of democracy with equalitarianism is an example. When the French Revolution proclaimed itself the champion of liberty, equality and fraternity it encouraged misconceptions about democracy that now rise to destroy it. The meaning of the word fraternity was clear: it was an ideal of human brotherhood to which even slave-owners could subscribe—as an ideal. The goal of liberty was familiar and its principles accepted by Americans, who had already been wrestling with the problem of how to reconcile liberty with order. But the word equality was ambiguous and explosive. The issue was ancient: Aristotle had recognized in the desire for equality one of the great problems of human society. The American Declaration had said that all men were created equal, but most of the men who said it and accepted it agreed that what it meant, and all that it could mean, was equality of opportunity and of civil rights. But the French revolutionaries acted as though they meant equality literally, and many Americans of the time accepted it thus. The results should have been instructive, for the French pursuit of social equality impaired the French quest for political freedom and ended in an emperor.

As a practical matter, no government can make or keep its citizens equal in ability, intelligence, character, influence

34

or possessions. Even if it could, the attempt would be at odds with the American convictions that society should be so fluid that a man may move upward through it, that unusual talent and initiative should bring unusual rewards, that from competition comes excellence. These beliefs predicate a society in which men neither start nor end equal in all respects. Competition means that someone must take second place, and that fact makes private enterprise and equalitarianism impossible bedfellows, for under the equalitarian theory no one must be in second place. Equalitarianism penalizes the more competent to please the less competent and, pushed to its logical extreme, could insist on making all men ignorant or miserable because some were so. In the complications of modern civilization an attempt to make and keep men really equal would require regimentation far beyond anything achieved by Hitler or Stalin. John Adams wrote in his *Defence of the Constitution:* "Nature, which has established in the universe a chain of being and universal order, has ordained that no two objects shall be perfectly alike. . . . there are inequalities which God and nature have planted there which no human legislature can ever eradicate."

Real democracy is an avenue along which men may march together toward their mutual elevation; it provides the opportunity but it cannot ensure or equalize the results. It is a practical plan, a reasoned form of government which allows for variations in human talents and desires. Equalitarianism is a vague dream of the idealist, a refuge of the weak and the frustrated, an appeal of the demagogue. No one has ever presented a workable blueprint for a permanent society maintaining full equality, and wherever seriously attempted it has ended in single leadership or chaos. Only a society susceptible to loose thinking and careless speech could confuse two concepts so irreconcilable. Few educated Americans seriously believe that the best man is he who is most like all other men, yet the idea has so permeated our national ethos that we accept slogans and developments that move society downward toward a dull level of the commonplace. De Tocqueville wrote: "Americans are so enamoured of equality that they would rather be equal in slavery than unequal in freedom."

This confusion between democracy as a road toward orderly individual excellence, and democracy as a free ride to effortless equality, has impaired the quality and effectiveness of American leadership. Yet every organized society needs leaders, and democracy most of all. No matter how great the political capacity of average men may be, they must implement their sovereignty by selecting trusted agents from among their ablest. The larger and more powerful the nation and the less its homogeneity of race, religion and inherited traditions, the greater its need for nurturing and accepting leadership of the highest quality. Democracy has no choice as to whether it will have leaders; its choice lies in the kind of leaders it wants and how it wants them to lead.

During the early decades of the American republic its leadership was exceptional in quality and aristocratic in spirit. The men who signed the Declaration meant to free themselves from British rule, but not to achieve social uniformity or to discard the traditions of culture they had inherited. Those traditions were part of themselves—as much theirs as Lord North's and more theirs than George the Third's—and implicit in them was political and cultural leadership by an element of society developed for that purpose. Though the democratic spirit of the new nation allowed no aristocracy of birth, the instinct and reason of its founders visualized a governing elite, which they themselves initially provided. They were conscious of their mental superiority over most of their countrymen, and revealed no inclination to hide it or to adjust their standards downward to the average level. Madison even went so far as to urge that special political privileges be given to those best qualified for statesmanship.

The last president in that aristocratic tradition was John Quincy Adams, whom few later statesmen equaled in mental and moral stature. Some, like Jackson, were natural leaders, but they did not possess or pretend superior cultivation or ethics. As popular sovereignty developed, politicians found it expedient to proclaim the political competence of the average American, and assure him that he was at least as good as anyone else. Even his cultural limitations were exalted to political virtues; his very average-ness became moral superiority; his untrained mind was translated into a treasury of basic Wordsworthian wisdom undefiled by patrician sophistries. Humble origin and simple manners became increasing political assets through the nineteenth century; they produced as presidents one Lincoln and several mediocrities.

In the twentieth century that tradition has had to be modified, but its spirit endures. A president must be or seem to be a typical American in attitude and manners. In real emergencies the voters will accept leaders of high talents, but they still want those talents to be housed in the frame and personality of a simple man of the people. To fill this difficult order often requires mutual pretense by the candidate and voter—a bit of deadpan play-acting by all concerned. Few contemporary candidates can claim to have been born in log cabins, but they are forgiven that lack of political foresight if they will grasp the nearest reasonable equivalent. Many a man's friends have not suspected how nobly humble were his origins until he became a candidate for political office. Mr. Harding had no difficulty in demonstrating that his background and standards were ordinary. Mr. Coolidge merely gave the log cabin tradition a Yankee salt box treatment. Mr. Hoover was an exception; he won the presidency as a specimen of the new American humanitarian efficiency expert—a symbolic pre-embodiment of Point Four—with no pretense of the commonplace; but he was never the choice of the politicians and failed of re-election. Franklin Roosevelt overcame the political handicap of being born a millionaire patroon by identifying himself with the Forgotten Man and by a talent for the Common Touch. When Wendell Willkie gained the nomination he reversed his progress; he went from Wall Street back to Ellwood, Indiana, and attempted in manner and accent the voice of the People. Mr. Truman, like Mr. Harding, did not need to be other than himself to seem on a happy level with the average in every way. In cultivation, manners and emotional reactions he was the symbol of those who disliked superiority. General Eisenhower recrossed the railroad tracks back to his Kansas boyhood and helped the voters to think of him more as Ike than as the great general, the friend of royalty and the President of Columbia University. To Adlai Stevenson, more than any recent candidate, should go credit for elevating the intellectual tone of national politics by the quality of his speeches, which were in striking contrast with those of his predecessor. But Mr. Truman's methods elected him in 1948 and Mr. Stevenson's methods failed him in 1952.

These adjustments of personality represent more than a continued deference to a waning frontier tradition. They go beyond politics and move into the psychological, revealing an ideal of leadership that the average American believes appropriate to democracy and consoling to his own ego. His unconscious reasoning is something like this:

"If we the people are indeed the sovereigns, then our statesmen are no more than our agents, to whom circumstances compel us to delegate great power. In order to be sure that they will use their power as we would use it, they should be men very like us in standards and reactions. We admire exceptional ability but trust ourselves to it only if it has the safe background of the commonplace. Our leaders should be men who literally talk our language." Mr. Truman talked their language before the 1948 election and Mr. Dewey, a man of recognized exceptional ability, did not.

Americans are also uncomfortable with leadership by superior men because subconsciously they fear it will make troublesome demands upon them. In the First World War they granted unprecedented powers to President Wilson, and in the crisis of the depression they gave a confident new president even greater ones, further extended after Pearl Harbor and retained for the Cold War. Thus for nearly forty years Americans have approved concessions of power to government beyond those to which their emotions and traditions were reconciled. They accepted the need for strong leadership but endured unhappily the demands it made upon them, and powerful leadership naturally associated itself in their minds with danger and sacrifice. Hence when immediate danger diminishes they yearn to relax from ideals and ardors and leadership back into their comfortable pursuit of the commonplace. Thus they vacillate between docility and assertiveness, between ideals and selfishness, between desiring and resenting the superior man.

Torn between regard for power in any form and fear of power in men, between dislike of being ordered and the mental ease of being led, between the tradition of self-reliance and eagerness not to miss any favors that government may be dispensing, American majorities have vacillated between granting their leaders great powers and protesting the forceful use of those powers. They have thus made consistent, constructive leadership almost impossible. This attitude extends even to the training of future leaders, where the majority gives lip service to education for leadership but exerts its influence in favor of education for equality.

It is clear that the political results of popular sovereignty are not as elevating as its advocates predicted. Their intention was to exalt both the power and the standards of the people, so that they could subordinate corruption and selfish interest groups. The actual effect upon government has been to make it bigger but not less corrupt, more difficult to control yet not less susceptible to pressures. Government has become a stronger master over individual men under guise of deferring to men collectively. **Popular** sovereignty has, paradoxically, led to increased authoritarianism by government in the name of the majority. The effect upon the people has been to make them satisfied with their current cultural standards, not striving toward higher ones.

Though one of the intentions of more power to the people was to eliminate special privilege, it has in practice widened the scope and competition for special favors from government. Group nepotism has moved from a trivial sin to a national habit and then to a recognized democratic principle. To ask for special favors—whether by tariff protection, aid to small business, price support for farmers, wage increase approvals for favored unions, an unusually profitable contract with government, or federal funds to finance some local ambition—these have become not only respectable but routine. Federal government has actually blessed the principle by itself operating under it, for until very recently cabinet officers in Labor, Agriculture and Commerce were the virtual agents of pressure interests in those fields.

Anarchy has become almost a forgotten word in America, but it is not a vanished danger. It merely takes new forms. The unscrupulous competition of special interests for government favors threatens to weaken the accredited government and substitute an invisible government that is not orderly, responsible or just. Pressure groups have harmed the nation less by the gains they got than by lowering political and ethical standards whenever they pass that way. The labor union that strikes against the public welfare, the corporation that seeks an exclusive monopoly or excessive protection against competition, the ubiquitous public relations counsel whose only morality is success in his mass inoculation of the public with any idea he is paid to promulgate, the irresponsible individual who breaks minor laws when he can get away with it, his brother who does not break the law but makes a joke of civic duty or any social ethic;—these men create an atmosphere of anarchy that is all the more dangerous because it is insidious and also profitable. Its cynicism infects society; its success attracts imitators.

All of this reveals the strident conflict between the historic principles of the American democratic tradition and the current American way of life. The stream of freedom has begun to run shallow and muddy. Until Americans decide whether they will risk their future to political expediency, or whether they will return to the political concepts and responsibilities of the founders, they will continue to wander in the frustrating maze of their own confusions.

5

Current Operations

*The belief that success is its own justification has pene-
trated the thought of our time.*
—L. T. HOBHOUSE, Democracy and Reaction.

*. . . in no other country is the ideal side of public life
so ignored by the mass and repudiated by its leaders.*
—JAMES BRYCE, The American Commonwealth.

BELIEVERS in popular sovereignty assume that it will
steadily lift the standards of citizens and their government. Their assumption rests on the conviction that men in
the mass are wiser and more virtuous than men in smaller
ruling groups; that the majority has political sagacity greater
than its components. Every move toward greater direct democracy has been advocated as a means to raise the standards of government and justice. Does popular sovereignty
really elevate the virtue of the state? The recent history of
America should throw light on that question.

The years from 1932 to 1953 are selected for consideration because they were a consistent period of government
policy and personnel, controlled by the majority as represented by a victorious Democratic Party. During that period
the New Deal began as an avowed movement to increase the
political power of the common man, and the Fair Deal maintained that profession. No other two administrations were
more deferential to the opinions and wishes of the majority
of American voters. In them, if anywhere in history, believers

42

in total democracy should expect to find improvement in the ethos of the people and in the ethics and quality of government.

They were highly controversial years, dominated by political figures who raised strong emotions in their admirers and opponents. No one who lived through them can judge them with complete detachment. It was a period of remarkable achievement, mixed with dangers, compromises and disillusions. Its social and economic gains are too well known to need recording here. Its weaknesses and questionable trends are less apparent and must be stated, not in partisan spirit but as relevant to ethical progress under popular sovereignty.

There is always some difference between ideals and practice, in nations as in persons. A wide divergence between the two, however, reflects not only upon the integrity of government but upon the ethics of the society that tolerates it. Recent and continuing discrepancies between the democratic ideal and the democratic performance have been disturbingly great. The same decades have also widened the gap between the traditions of various democracies and the current opinions of many of their citizens.

In Britain the historical dynastic and religious significance of the last coronation ceremonies contrasts with the current political ideas of most of its people. In France the tradition of powerful centralized government is at variance with the reality of unstable political fragmentation. In the Netherlands, centuries of Protestant nonconformity and commercial *laissez faire* provide curious foundations for a modern highly organized state now dominated by the Catholic and Socialist parties. In America, rapid and controversial changes have left a broad gap between the traditional ideals and the current practices of the people. Though complete deference to tradition would prevent progress, such emphatic discrepancies between inherited and current thinking bring confusions and frustrations to society and individuals. These discrepancies derive from many causes, but certainly one of the chief of them is ignorance or disregard of earlier standards and values by the increasingly dominant common man.

Citizens who blame a federal administration for its failure to approximate the democratic ideal assume that by electing other officers of government that failure can be remedied. Some of the defects of recent administrations were indeed of their own making, but many of them reflected conflicts in a society which was losing its way, uncertain of what it wanted of government and itself. Democracy's departure from clearly envisioned objectives to the crab-like motions of political opportunism was not the work of a single man or political party, just as the expansion in the size and power of government was due to more than the leaders of the New Deal. They were influenced by popular desires and world events as well as by their own political philosophy, and an administration committed to reduce big government will find itself forced by similar circumstances to continue it. From his long political experience Senator Smoot formulated "Smoot's Law" that the cost of government tends in a democracy to increase annually, no matter what party is in power. Those who expect that the new administration can notably alter the course or size of government ignore the trends of democracy, the strength of world forces and the lessons of history. What concerns us here is whether popular sovereignty inevitably means opportunistic government, or whether it can achieve an elevated and orderly policy and society. The crux of that matter lies in the character of the average American, for he is now king.

The ideal citizen would possess mature cultural and ethical ideals as well as political ones. He would have had the kind of education that gave him historical perspective and social restraint; he would have an understanding of the limitations

44

as well as the proper uses of democratic government, a strong sense of personal civic responsibility, courage to differ from the majority, and inner defenses against emotional appeals. If this hypothetical citizen, multiplied by millions to make up the ruling majority, were called upon to decide only major political policies, his decisions would be as wise as human fallibility permits. The real average voter falls somewhat short of those qualifications. In spite of that fact he not only renders verdicts on major political policies but upon issues beyond and beneath them. The expansion of government into nearly every aspect of his life results in his determination of questions beyond his present capacity.

The first great expansion of American government was to inject itself into the nation's economic activities. As industry developed, the political freedoms guaranteed by the Constitution seemed to many Americans inadequate without protection against economic exploitation and insecurity. They demanded that federal government regulate and even operate industry. For several decades the nation has been going through the pains of subordinating its economic system to its political democracy. Free enterprise has been transformed into government-guided enterprise, and though government has not abolished the market place as the determinant of economic values, it has set new rules and closely oversees the competition. Society now accepts the principle that even in peacetime government may decide who is to produce what, and how much, and sell it at what price.

Just as guarantees of political freedom seemed to many citizens inadequate without detailed economic regulation by government, both then appeared ineffective unless government also gained control over general social welfare. Once the principle of the social responsibility of federal government was embarked upon, no one knew where it should, or could, stop. The great depression accelerated the process of government intervention in private problems, for it produced a flood of new demands upon federal government. Hungry men out of work were not concerned with political theory or the proper boundaries of government's responsibility and power, but with immediate bread and jobs. These they demanded, and got, from government. Their demands were chiefly economic, but they created habits of mind and attitudes that went beyond economics. Modern democracy has accepted literally the theory that government has the obligation to help the private citizen solve his personal problems, whether they be of housing, health, employment or education. As early as 1935 the results of a questionnaire indicated that 76.8 per cent of Americans favored the idea that it is the duty of the state to see that every person who wants a job should have one.

When social reform or the democratization of some established institution moved too slowly to suit them, many Americans turned to federal government to speed the process or even to take over the function. By its frequent acquiescence government further increased in size, complexity, power and expense, and society and the state have become almost the same thing in America. Recent years have even seen the economic responsibilities of our federal government carried beyond national boundaries, for many men of other continents have come to regard America as morally pledged to provide them, too, with security and welfare. Yet, by human paradox, the more widely the democratic state has ranged, the less clear has become its voice; the greater the responsibility for human welfare federal officials have assumed collectively, the less they have met that responsibility as individuals. By trying to achieve simultaneous attention over so expanded a field, our statesmen and voters have not found it humanly possible to give adequate attention to any one major problem. To a vestigial devotee of the theory that the best government is the one which governs least, our highly centralized democracy seems to be creating Narcissism at its center and frustration at its periphery.

These expansions of the democratic function brought revisions in its social order. They altered balances of power within society, elevating some classes and depressing others. The interests of some "forgotten men" were notably advanced, but in the process other men and women, like the small-fixed-salary-earner and the annuity-holder, were newly forgotten. By moving in as umpire in economic disputes, government not only disturbed the relatively free operation of supply and demand, but made decisions that had social implications far beyond the particular economic issue at stake. The result has been to make national economics subject to partisan politics and to stress the conflicts of interests between economic classes as a political issue.

Such steps helped to turn democracy from a form of government into a social philosophy and an overall culture, amorphous but insistent. Since a culture is more powerful than a political creed it enables American society, in the name of democracy, to apply almost irresistible extra-political pressures upon individuals, nearly always in the direction of conformity with popular opinion. Every society has used social sanctions, but never before has a free society urged them so powerfully upon its members over so broad and varied a field. To some conservatives and nonconformists (and the situation has ironically made the two almost identical) the popular majority seems to be developing an insistence which threatens a new kind of social tyranny in the name of democratic freedom.

Government itself has on occasion deferred so abjectly to pressure groups that it has almost failed to govern, but has merely waited to see to which of the conflicting interests it must this time defer. Once caught in this dilemma of post-

ponement and oscillation, a statesman ceases to be a statesman and becomes only a rather desperate extemporizer.
Individual voters during the Roosevelt and Truman administrations found themselves confused as to their own
functions amid these unofficial operations, and wondered
whether their citizen's functions were not almost nullified by
this jockeying between pressure groups and government.
Many a voter naturally decided that his only political effectiveness rested in his support of whatever pressure group
best represented his economic interests. A newcomer to democracy might see it as a competition among free citizens to
get all they can from one another and give as little as possible in return.

At what level, for example, shall the government maintain
the prices of farm products? The decision rests upon an
analysis of all the complications of the voting power of the
farm bloc *versus* the reactions to increased retail food prices
by the urban consumer, who also has a vote. Will crucial
elections to Senate and House be won by deferring to the
labor union vote in Detroit or the farm vote in Iowa? The
interests of other citizens are ignored, and the innocent by-
stander is the man who gets hurt. The system cheapens and
often circumvents the proper democratic process.

It also diminishes the stature and responsibility of the
private citizen. With labor, agriculture and industry setting
the pace in pressure politics, private citizens begin to look
for pressure groups which will support their own personal
interests. If they can find none, they expect their own representatives in federal and state capitals to put their local interests before all else. There is nothing new in this practice
except that it has now attained the dignity of a serious democratic theory. Under that theory the best congressman is the
man who gets the most for his supporters. If the practice of
that theory became general, the elected representative would

be merely the messenger boy of his district, and the ideal congressman would be a composite of an adding machine, a Gallup poll and a super-lobbyist. His character and judgment would be irrelevant to the practice of his high office, and few self-respecting men would accept nomination to it.

The expansion of government and of popular sovereignty did not bring control of bureaucracy, but added new problems to its functioning. The numbers of government employees mounted more than their quality. Responsible power is what keeps free men free, but the greater and more complicated the administrative machine became, the more comfortably remote it made both its bureaucrats and its citizens from direct responsibility for their actions. To keep the machine in operation was often the chief collective motive of the personnel of a department; to keep his own job in existence and himself in it was the chief personal motivation of many a government employee. Cause and effect of office actions were reassuringly obscured by the numbers of those involved; mistakes or dishonesty were less easily traced to their originators when nobody made a final decision but many attached their initials. Some federal employees functioned as though cautious time-serving promised promotion more surely than hard work or initiative; as though anonymity was the best policy. Loyalties of underlings were often confused or devious; some who were in career service disobeyed or circumvented orders from their immediate chiefs, whom they thought might be temporary, and took secret instructions from party politicians or others who might be powerful friends later on.

This structural irresponsibility corrupts moral responsibility. At higher levels of government service were, quite naturally, men with personal ambition. There is nothing wrong with personal ambition in government service; indeed, without it the quality of government would be still

49

lower. But to rise through ability and moral courage is one thing, to rise by studied sycophancy or "playing the angles" is quite another. Many ambitious bureaucrats concluded that the way to power was to ride along with one's fellows until the propitious moment came to leap to power. In their decisions on matters of national importance, expediency outweighed other considerations. A government partly run by officials who are acquiescent until their time comes to be dictatorial is not likely to be one of consistent high policy or high morale.

The vast administrative machine itself has an impersonality that gives it a mechanical self-direction. Consistent with physical law, it keeps relentlessly moving because it is in motion, or remains inert because it has not moved. Men who should be directing its operations merely ride on it, and its mechanics become an army of busy and competing people certain of procedures but uncertain of ends. Problems are resolved in a random conflict of force against force, of ambition against ambition, while the machine grinds on almost independent of the purpose for which it was created—if that is remembered at all. Two laws seem to apply to this bureaucracy: that in its service mediocrity drives out excellence, and that as it expands its aims deteriorate and its morality declines.

A former member of the State Department wrote of it in 1944: "The Department is an unbelievably inefficient organization. It is not run. It just jerks along. Foreign policy is in the hands of whichever of two dozen higher officers is able at any moment and by any means to seize the ball. But in the State Department there are queer rules: when a player seizes the ball and makes for the goal line, all the members of his team are entitled to tackle him. As often as not the ball is seized and not carried over any goal line but hidden under the back steps." The description would apply with considerable validity to some other departments of government.

All governments are more or less opportunist, and the wheels of democracy in particular must be greased by politicians. They serve an essential function, but if their opportunism is too dominant government loses its direction as well as its character. John Bright once said that he had known the British Parliament to do some good things, but he never knew it to do a good thing because it was a good thing—yet in comparison to most other legislative bodies the British Parliament of his time was a deliberative body of the highest order. Democracy must be prepared to endure opportunism from its public servants but it cannot accept it as the determinant principle of government. Yet the American federal government of recent years made expediency in many areas of its operations an accepted routine. Leaders like Mr. Roosevelt and Mr. Truman, who had special flairs for opportunism, set the tone and developed many willing and able imitators. With pragmatism the national philosophy, it is not surprising that one man of cabinet rank could in 1951 assure another that "in Washington whatever a man gets away with is usually Okay with the Boss."

The public during those years seemed to accept anything short of major corruption with a shrug, and only sporadically showed concern about ethical standards in government. This was in contrast with George Washington, who demonstrated that it was possible to make moral authority a strong weapon of democracy—that democratic leadership can be something more than deference to mass society, or the alternative of riding herd over it. Now that America has been called on as never before to give the world moral leadership it has failed to provide it in any consistent way, or to set an example by its management of its own internal affairs. American leadership since the first World War has vacillated between reluctance and forcefulness, and its diplomacy has been tinged with the attitude of a small boy eager to get home and drop his party manners. We have been lucky to find qualified leadership when we have most needed it, but the supply will always be sporadic and inadequate so long as the day-to-day practices of society and government fail to breed it.

America's position in world affairs would be more effective if foreign nations had not observed the scandals and ethical compromises of the American government at home. The paradoxes of a department of justice under investigation for the selling of injustice, and of inquisitions of private citizens in the name of freedom have not been national assets abroad. Only in the perspective of history will later citizens be able to estimate how corroding has been the influence of political opportunism on the standards of the nation. It is tragic that two recent presidents were so ready to ignore or condone the low ethical tone of some of their close associates. Mr. Roosevelt not only tolerated the Huey Longs, Crumps and Hagues but played up to them when political occasion made it expedient. He used government power and government allocation of funds to win political support, and did so with jaunty cynicism. Mr. Truman's defense of the moral obliquity of some of his leading appointees on the grounds that they had done nothing demonstrably illegal needs no elaboration here. If he would not turn his back on his friends, he was ready to let them turn their backs on the moral dignity of government. Mr. Eisenhower has sadly missed opportunities to raise the ethical level of government by clean-cut and unequivocal positions against the dissemination of half-truths and false charges by men of his own party and sometimes of his own choosing. He cannot be forever excused on grounds of political expediency, party unity or his own naïveté. Shabby means to gain party ends are defended as justified by the ends in view, but that defense only reveals how widespread has become the ethical confusion of American society.

Cynicism and moral flabbiness were not however invented by recent political leaders. Describing the state of federal government previous to 1933 in the official report of the Hoover Commission, Professor Charles E. Merriam wrote of "the rapid spread of graft and corruption in old and new forms," of "a system in which the pillars of virtue may become chief corruptionists," of "the distrust approaching contempt in some instances for politicians and government," of "a widespread breakdown of the former integrity of the federal service," and of "the lack of confidence in the processes of the courts and especially of the flabby administration of criminal justice."

When the Hoover Commission reported, the numbers and costs of government had not mounted to their recent heights. Walter Lippmann, in his column for December 2, 1952, approached the question of government ethics from the special angle of federal self-inflation:

"The fatty degeneration of government is a serious disease. . . . The Truman administration is a bad case of fatty degeneration. As time went on the administration has acquired more and more powers and has spent more and more money but it has had less and less control over the use of that power and that money. . . . To correct these troubles it will be necessary to do more than reorganize the structure of the government. It will be necessary to set up . . . certain standards of public conduct. . . . The predominant problems here are those of morals and discipline."

Yet what was the reaction of the average citizen toward a president, leading members of whose administration were under investigation for unethical practices? For five consecutive years the American Institute of Public Opinion asked a cross-section of American citizens this question:

"What man that you have heard of or read about, living today in any part of the world, do you admire the most?"

In 1951 President Truman received the third largest number of votes. In 1952, when press and radio were almost daily reporting new disclosures of dubious practices by men for whom he was responsible, he was the fourth most admired man in the world, by Americans who voted in the poll.

This episode is offered not to add to the discredit of an ex-president, but because it raises questions as to the ethical values of the American public. Did the citizens in the poll not know of the Washington scandals, or did they know and not care? Was it due to gross ignorance or moral indifference? Had Jefferson's plowman and professor alike lost their judgments on moral issues? However one tries to explain the poll the light it throws upon the first question in this chapter—whether popular sovereignty elevates the virtue of the state and its citizens—is hardly reassuring.

American popular sovereignty cherishes a high opinion of its own virtue, and its conscience is seldom tender about its own actions or omissions. When flaws appear in its government, popular society promptly draws a distinction between its chosen officials and itself, and seeks the causes in the deterioration of public servants or of the machinery of government—never in its own. Confucius commented: "The superior man blames himself; the inferior man blames others."

We often remark that the current problems in France derive from the irresponsibility of its electorate; that Mussolini and Hitler could not have risen to power if the peoples of those countries had not lost their moral ethos—but we do not bring the lesson home. When roused to action, we conceive no better method than to investigate and prosecute individuals, and in the last analysis to throw the rascals out. They may be guilty, but simply to punish their guilt does not end the influences that created it. This way of dealing with social and political decay is palliative and not remedial, and it sometimes smears the reputations of the innocent, or punishes the minnows while the sharks escape.

Both minnows and sharks come from the people and go back to feed upon them. They could not have got into government if society had not tolerated within itself the ethical miasma on which they breathe. The heart of the problem lies in the ideals and practices of the sovereign people.

When average men became the sovereigns of the state they assumed exacting political responsibilities which even those who thought most highly of their competence believed barely within their scope. Since then, average men have added to their political power and thus expanded their political responsibilities, but failed to meet them in a responsible way. They have not realized that the quality of government depends upon their personal standards. Instead of bringing their private decencies into their public affairs, Americans have allowed low public standards to infect their private code. Until the common man personally confronts the magnitude of the duties he has assumed; until he insists upon quality in cultural as well as political leadership and therefore in himself, the practice of democracy will belie its promise.

6

The Voice of the People

*It is a besetting vice of democracies to substitute pub-
lic opinion for law. That is the usual form in which
masses of men exhibit their tyranny. . . . Men in
America are thought to be more under control of
extra-legal authorities, and to defer more to those
around them . . . than in almost any other country.*
                    —JAMES FENIMORE COOPER.

*Public opinion . . . seems to be a mixture of sense
and nonsense, of prejudice, of more or less clearly defined feelings coming from influences . . . of sentiment rather than . . . judgment.*
                    —JEREMIAH W. JENKS,
                    The Guidance of Public Opinion.

THE VOICE of the people is the chorus of democracy,
asserting the collective freedom of men. There is no
more majestic political concept than that of citizens recording their individual opinions with confidence that whatever
the verdict of the majority it will be accepted by all. America's application of that concept for nearly two centuries
has been the admiration of the world.

The official mandates of the people to their government
are spoken through the ballot box. There the people speak
responsibly; each voter feels that for the moment he per-
sonifies democracy. But the people as voters do not speak
frequently or always clearly, and if that were the only way
in which their voices could be heard, modern democratic

government would falter. The ballot offers the citizen little opportunity to give definite opinions on all the numerous and complicated issues of the hour, and it is difficult to see how it could do so. The voter casts his ballot for a list of persons whose positions on national issues are not always clear or irrevocable. It is true that each group of candidates represents a political party which has a platform on major issues, but party platforms are notoriously vague and jerry-built, and the partisan climate of election day is not ideal for the determination of high principles in national policy. As a clear and direct expression on specific issues the official mandate of the people is of limited value.

The limitations which confront both voters and elected candidates were illustrated by the 1952 election. The issues upon which unequivocal opinions of the people were then desirable included the Korean War, policies toward Russia and China, aid to Europe, the federal budget and tax structure, economic controls, and the size of government. The ballot gave no opportunity for the voter to express a direct personal verdict on any of these issues. But the difficulty did not lie wholly in the limitations of the ballot. There are human limitations too. Even if the ballot offered citizens a chance to express themselves on all major issues, many voters would have subordinated them to preferences in political parties, or in the personalities of the leading candidates, or to some immediate local interest. The limitations of the official voice of the people lie in the intellects of the voters as well as in the mechanics of the ballot.

To overcome the mechanical difficulties at least; to learn what his fellow-citizens want him to do, a president must consequently find ways to supplement the ballot. He can send up trial balloons, but this is a risky and somewhat hypocritical method and is rarely practical. He can wait two years to see whether the congressional elections favor his party, and from their results draw whatever inferences he can. Through conversation, travel and reports he can gather opinions, but not all of them are balanced, authoritative or disinterested. Recent presidents have supplemented all these devices by augmenting the White House staff concerned with estimating and reporting to him the reactions of the people. All of these methods are however secondary to his greatest source of public opinion—the voluntary daily self-expression of citizens through countless spoken, printed and recorded media. The national will emerges more fully from this informal public debate than from formal elections. It is the unofficial voice of the people, and it is not hard for men in public life to hear—indeed, they cannot escape its clamor. Their problem is to determine whether what they hear is considered, informed and representative and how much they should defer to it.

To the statesman this strident popular voice is a compass, to the politician it is an order. Its conclusions often anticipate the ballot, which merely verifies them after the fact. It expresses itself on issues which the ballot does not cover, and it is continuous where the ballot is only occasional. It is less partisan than the decisions of election days. As the forum of society, the melting pot of public opinion, this popular Babel is the real mandate and safeguard of democracy.

In some respects it is also a liability to good government. Though it is not difficult to hear it is often difficult to interpret. Sometimes its noise keeps public men from doing their own thinking. With casual half-knowledge it often creates climates of opinion that determine decisions before the facts are clear. It is often the victim of its own emotions and confusions. Inchoate and volatile, it can be irresponsible and undependable.

Part of the inadequacy of public opinion arises from the random way in which it is formed. No one knows all the ingredients that go into its melting pot, or how pure they are, or what chemical reactions they will create, or what men may be stirring the brew. Trivial words and events may be more determinative than important ones: in the final crystallization of public opinion the views of a taxi driver may influence more people than those of an editor; a pertinent quip by a Will Rogers or Bob Hope may be more potent than a national broadcast by a cabinet member. The emergent conclusions are a blend of conscious thought and unconscious reactions. Men and women can seldom state clearly what factors determine their decisions on most issues, but in many cases a desire to agree with men they like or to disagree with men they dislike plays a considerable part. The fact that so little is known about how public opinion is formed makes its power, its irrationality and the possibilities of its misuse a little frightening.

The collective power of press, radio and television over the minds of the people increases yearly. They aid public opinion to crystallize more quickly and government to respond to it more promptly. This is an advantage in a crisis like Pearl Harbor, but in many cases a quick and emotional decision is likely to be a regrettable one. Not only do modern media for communication accelerate popular decisions but their public potency makes them targets for every kind of propaganda and influence. The more powerful they become, the more men who seek power seek to control them, sometimes by dubious methods. Others, whether politicians, reformers, industrialists or labor leaders, sometimes court their good will with a sycophancy that is not healthy for themselves or for society.

Though American public opinion is far superior to mob sentiment, it has some of the characteristics of crowd psychology. No single person can be held responsible for the voice of the people and it therefore rarely represents the most elevated reactions of the individuals who compose it. The anonymity of being only a member of the crowd invites men to express reactions they would hesitate to display elsewhere. Multiplied by millions, it is the reaction of the individual citizen that forms public opinion and hence public policy. How then does the average man make up his mind? His mental process has been described by an eminent sociologist thus:

"He is dominated by routine and tradition. His philosophy consists for the most part of conventional principles that are provided by pulpit, party or counting house. On the whole he is suspicious of ideas, especially if they be new: thinking is irksome and largely unnecessary since he finds that a judicious regard for what 'they say' will solve most of his problems. The political 'spell-binder' and the professional reformer, to whose interest it is to study his idiosyncrasies, find that a skilful appeal to his prejudices or to his fixed ideas never fails to bring a favorable response. On the whole he prefers orthodoxy to scholarship in his minister, loyalty to party rather than political wisdom in his statesmen, and the preservation of a profitable status quo in his business."

This description hardly flatters the average American, but nearly every one of us is recognizable in some part of it. As a picture of the average voter it is excessively critical. It was written some twenty years ago and recent decades have brought some relaxations of orthodoxy and many examples of independent thinking. Men and women are meeting daily across the United States for various civic purposes, and many of them reveal genuine efforts to escape from self-interest and prejudice and to search sincerely for more flexible points of view in themselves as well as in others. But unfortunately such men and women are not quite average. The American public as a whole is slow to be aroused and easily diverted, emotional and sporadic in its thinking, tending to personalize whatever it considers, and interested only when events are dramatized, simplified and presented on an either-or basis. "It ain't so much the people's ignorance that does the harm," said Artemus Ward, "as their knowin' so much that ain't so."

Who interprets the voice of the people is almost as important as what inspires it. There are many interpreters in press, radio and politics, and a considerable number of them are well-informed and fair-minded. The radio, which otherwise has much to answer for, has done society good service in providing a few commentators of high quality and reasonable detachment. Such men serve democracy well, but they are outnumbered by the second rate and the biased.

There are also nebulous groups of men who analyze and interpret public opinion—many of them as official or unofficial appendages to various offices of the federal government. Their quality and motivations are often dubious. These interpreters, advisors and front men, often without direct or personal responsibility, have influenced both officials and public beyond their mental or ethical qualifications. Their behind-the-door position lends itself to slanted reports, political chicanery, propaganda twists and personal log-rolling. Some of these men serve useful and valid ends, but as a group they probably distort and mislead. It is questionable whether these semi-professional mental bodyguards and hatchet men are an asset to government.

What has been said applies to the political aspects of public opinion, but the voice of the people is also dominant in nearly every other area of national life. There is no segment of thought in which it does not feel qualified to render a verdict, and thus determine the culture of the nation. How well is it qualified to do so? The crucial tests of its maturity are the values it sets and its attitude toward the individual. The mature voice of the people would assert not only the political and economic freedom of man, but the cultural freedom and importance of the individual man. It would demonstrate the restraint necessary to leave the individual free to develop his talents in his own way, in a social environment which guided him only by its own high standards of ethics and quality. It would not press him toward conformity, for it would recognize that to do so would make sterile the seed-bed of its own cultural progress. American public opinion does not meet those tests. It does not happily tolerate the individual who challenges majority views or customs. It does not surround him with an atmosphere of mature cultural values. It is suspicious of originality and often resentful of challenge.

In his analysis of character and opinion in the United States, Santayana wrote:

". . . there is no country in which people live under more overpowering compulsions. . . . What is exacted cuts deeper [than what is prohibited]; it creates habits which overlay nature; and every faculty is atrophied that does not conform with them. Even what is best in American life is compulsory, —the idealism, the zeal, the beautiful unison of the great movements. You must wave, you must cheer, you must push with the irresistible crowd: otherwise you will feel like a traitor, a soulless outcast, a deserted ship high and dry upon the shore. . . . The national faith and morality are vague in idea but inexorable in spirit. . . . in a country where all men are free, every man finds that what most matters has been settled for him beforehand."

In a society so self-conscious and eager for unity, individual uniqueness and the free play of ideas cannot be preserved by the Constitution and courts alone. By extra-legal devices the majority can undermine the self-expression of the original or nonconformist. When this is done by lynching mobs or Vigilantes society recognizes the menace, for even when

62

such groups break no laws they are clearly contrary to the spirit of free men. But when some more reputable group with some more generally admired objective forces its concept on others by similar pressures—pressures not illegal but not in the spirit of freedom, society fails to see that the danger is equal because the method is the same. Any American has the right to try to persuade others to adopt his way of thought, for persuasion is the essence of democracy. But he must use no methods, legal or illegal, contrary to the spirit of free men. To go beyond pure persuasion by threatening or hinting some social or economic penalty for failure to accept the general philosophy, is to offend that spirit. Democracy does not vest in any self-appointed men the right to use any kind of threat or duress—even the threat of social stigma—to force another to accept their ideas. Where legal safeguards against such insidious coercion do not exist, respect for the integrity of the spirit of personal freedom must apply. This principle is basic to true democracy, for social sanctions, unscrupulously applied, can be as compelling as guns. Truth can emerge only after its free individual pursuit, and must not become what Mr. Justice Holmes once lightly defined it to be: the majority vote of that nation that can lick all others.

This is true even when those who attempt the coercion are leading citizens working for a good cause. Yet in a thousand little ways the freedom of the individual to be different is challenged by just such men. Though the men of the press and the academic profession have been quick to protest when their freedom of speech is attacked, they have not been equally alert to recognize and oppose the challenges to freedom that occur every time an individual reluctantly yields to some social pressure because he fears he will suffer in some way if he does not.

Such pressures are so familiar that we seldom recognize them for what they are. Suppose (and the supposition is not fanciful) that in a city where all the best citizens generously support the Community Chest, a prosperous newcomer declines to contribute. Suppose that several leading business men then inform him that unless he gives, and gives a specific sum they have determined to be appropriate, he and his family will not be "welcomed" into the clubs and private schools of the area, and that he and his business associates "cannot count on the cooperation" of the local banks and industries. Has the man the right to refuse to be generous to a good cause? Have leading citizens the right to threaten him with economic penalties or social Coventry for declining to be a good citizen by their specific definition? If coercion is justified in that case, who is to determine in what other cases it can also be justified? Yet such practices, often in polite intangible forms, are general in America. The noble end is assumed to justify the means.

Thomas Paine said that government is made necessary by the inability of moral virtue to govern the world unassisted. The ideal government would be one of few laws but a general deference to public opinion. But such deference would be good government only if public opinion were so enlightened that it would apply its great power to individuals only with the utmost circumspection. American society has not yet reached that level of enlightenment; it has not yet the wisdom or restraint to govern by social sanctions. It has not yet learned to distinguish between socially-valuable nonconformity and dangerous subversion, or how to investigate possible challenges to freedom without endangering freedom. Too often it creates an atmosphere in which the individual conforms because his power to envisage the possibility of nonconformity has been sapped from him by the enervating air of social conformity he has breathed so

64

long. Many Americans hold secret or disguise their real opinions if they are unpopular; others discard their personal opinions because they cannot believe them to be really valid if they differ from the accepted ones. The price for those kinds of intellectual pacifism is the loss of moral courage and mental self-respect.

As disseminators of public opinion the American press presents examples of the best and worst possible standards. Unfortunately the devotees of the bad standards greatly outnumber those of the good. A handful of American journals are unexcelled in news coverage and general distinction. The quality and skill of their best international correspondents like James Reston are envied by other nations, and the columns of a few men like Walter Lippmann are high-water marks in the history of journalism. But the average quality of the American newspaper and newspaper man is so low that it is cheapening American thought and standards.

It has been said of one of the nation's greatest newspapers that in every issue there is learning and lubricity, piety and pornography, and all of it decorated with astoundingly good photographs, and Matthew Arnold wrote: "If one were searching for the best means to efface and kill in a whole nation the discipline of respect, the feeling for what is elevated, one could not do better than take the American newspapers." Even Arnold might lack words to describe the tabloids and movie magazines that have spawned and flourished since he wrote. A special Congressional committee reported on December 2, 1952, that an "incredible volume" of filthy literature is flooding the nation's newsstands, and called on publishers to clean house before an outraged public demands that the industry be regulated by government. The committee said that the salacious paper-bound books, "girlie magazines" and so-called comic books (of which some ninety million are read each month) have become a serious menace to the nation. But the public seems more delighted than outraged, and its taste and value-judgments presumably decline further with each new daily dose of commercialized vulgarity.

The issue is not simply one of the glorification of sex and crime. At a time when Americans need, as never before, all the accurate information they can get about their nation and the world, much important news in press and over the air is kaleidoscoped (and often distorted in the process) to leave room or time for the trivial and the commercial. The American press as a whole is not supplying American citizens with the accurate facts they need, or even utilizing the news that comes to them through the excellent press services. Its daily spate of mediocrity may be more harmful than its lurid and filthy products, for its constant cheapness of tone lowers the reader's standards before he is aware of what has happened to him. There is less yellow journalism than in the past, but more that is pallid and purple. The radio rarely equals the press in the sensational and the dirty, but exceeds it in the sentimental and the trivial. There is little to choose between them, and the average television program is certainly no better.

The results are not only directly upon the minds of a hundred million consumers but upon their habits. Many Americans spend so much time in sodden absorption in radio, television and press that little is left for other communication or recreation. Inner resources for self-entertainment are atrophying from lack of use, and personal thought is being made unnecessary by the acceptance of predigested opinion from favorite commentators. Communication of general ideas, even between members of the same family, has declined, and conversation has degenerated. How can it be otherwise when innumerable Americans spend hours each

66

week sitting mindlessly motionless before canned entertainment which is, in the words of Louis Kronenberger, "riddled with the imbecilities of announcers and splotched with the timidities of sponsors?" It is not only a question of what our media of communication do but of what they fail to do. Think how much the press and radio could have elevated public taste and knowledge over the past thirty years! The difference between their potential and their actual performance is a measure of their failure.

A long time ago a man of deep understanding said that humanity's progress lay in fixing attention on whatsoever things are true, honorable, just, lovely and of good report. Most of the American media of communication seem devoted to fixing public attention on whatsoever things are trivial, ugly, vulgar, salacious and of ill report—as though they were consciously exploiting for profit the lowest depths of human nature. Those who control these media say that they must faithfully report the American scene; that whatever the public wants to know is news and that the public wants the lurid; that however much they may personally deplore public taste they are not in business for their health. They are certainly not in business for the mental health of the American people as they now operate, yet their profits are made in a democracy which allows them freedom because it assumes they will advance public welfare. Press and radio are more than mirrors of American life; they can raise or lower public standards more than ministers, priests, teachers or legislators. Their power over national thought should make them feel the responsibilities of *noblesse oblige*. The influence of the news makes its dissemination as crucial a public service as water, light and transportation—indeed more so, since press and radio feed and move the minds of citizens and not their bodies. They cannot escape a public duty to give the average man the best, not the worst, he will stand for.

In the early days of the republic, the voice of the people gained unity from their common racial heritage and cultural aspirations. The time has passed when American society has that kind of solidarity, and it cannot be arbitrarily created again. It must achieve another kind of unity through devotion to the free and respected diversity of a society with mingled races, traditions and ideas, but with common devotion to freedom and human elevation. That kind of diversity means an orderly battle-royal of ideas, with every citizen either a participant or an ardent spectator. Democracy must see to it that when truth emerges victor it will be honored and followed. Truth cannot emerge without free communication of this sort; it also cannot emerge if those who should spread it let it become muddied into half-truth.

Since the people's voice is so compelling, the citizens who compose it must understand their part in it, and the parts of others. Their sense of responsibility must equal their sense of power. All the forces of society must contribute to strengthening the ability of the average citizen to distinguish between sincerity and demagoguery, between fact and opinion, between truth and half-truth, between what uplifts and what degrades him.

How to hear and interpret the voice of the people, how citizens can help one another to make that voice uplifting, how they can keep it from being dominated by the powerful few or the intolerant many—these are perennial problems of democracy. They become ever more crucial as the *vox populi* becomes more strident and irresponsible.

7

Acceleration and Inertia

Democracy is an infinite mass of conflicting minds and conflicting interests . . . which loses in collective intellectual energy in proportion to the perfection of its expansion.
—BROOKS ADAMS,
The Degradation of the Democratic Dogma.

PREVIOUS CHAPTERS have considered the political aspects of popular sovereignty. They reach the conclusion that if the voice of the people is to determine so directly the actions of government, there must be adjustments in its machinery and a clearer understanding of the meaning and responsibilities of democratic citizenship. Since the values of a society as a political organism are inseparable from its values as a culture, the key to good government by the people is a devotion to high quality in its culture. The rest of this book is therefore concerned with the quality and values of American society, and an analysis of the forces that are working to elevate and to debase them.

Throughout the centuries philosophers have tried to discern some basic laws to guide men's collective future. What they have concluded their fellow men have not always acted upon, and human society grinds its wayward course without much attention to abstract principles. Events make mockery of human reason. Yet the hope of mankind rests on bringing order and understanding into human action; upon

69

becoming the master and not the victim of events. The realization of this hope demands more than the control of physical forces, for without the balance wheel of moral mastery they only augment man's power for self-destruction. Unless modern free society can renew its ethical impulse, it will lose moral energy as it expands and will follow the cycle of human life to ultimate decay.

These alternatives are brought alarmingly near by the quickening of man's conquest of physical power. The rate of that conquest has accelerated almost beyond our control as events mass, charge themselves and explode upon men's unready minds and spirits. When an army makes a rapid advance into new territory, its general is likely to call a halt to survey the scene and consolidate the gains; to bring up a balanced force that can hold the conquered ground. Free society has rushed into unfamiliar territory and its ground troops have outrun their cultural supplies. They are in danger of spreading out too thinly, of losing sight of their final objective, even of losing themselves unless new maps are provided. Since in the march of democracy every man is a general, no single leader can call a halt in our material progress and bring up supporting cultural reserves. Only democratic society itself can do that, and its failure to do so may bring its own destruction. With all its intelligence and organization, the army of democracy has made no adequate provision to develop spiritual forces to support its material and scientific advance. It has concentrated on tactics not strategy, on expediency not consolidation.

In 1900 Henry Adams learned at the International Exposition something of the potential power of modern science in the form of the new dynamo. He accepted the inevitability of this new force and saw its potential service to man, but he feared the amorality of its power in a new world which would have no common scale of measurement with the older one, and in which men might be the victims of the chance collisions of physical forces. Adams spent the rest of his life trying to find a basis for unity between the dynamo and the older energy of the human spirit. He never found it, and society is still searching.

Adams did gain glimmerings of a law governing the rate of society's acceleration, and predicted that a great collision of uncontrolled forces would take place by mid-century. Mid-century has come, the collision seems imminent, and the recently demonstrated power of the hydrogen bomb make the results a thousand times more devastating than Adams could have dreamed. The acceleration which alarmed him in 1900 has been dwarfed by the speed with which the world now hurtles down the ringing grooves of change. Never was man in such imbalance between his physical power and his spiritual frailty. The collisions of the new forces—economic as well as scientific—are still by chance, for he has found no guiding reconciliation between the humane culture of the old world and the mechanical culture of the new. It is not difficult to guess the end of a society in which this imbalance continues.

The chance of free society to escape the final crash depends, of course, upon whether the spirit of man can master the results of his own conquest of nature or whether, like a pilot who blacks out by too sudden acceleration, he will lapse into spiritual inertness. This is a familiar alternative even to those who have not read Spengler, Ortega and Toynbee, but though the problem is obvious it has never been faced squarely by American society. If the spiritual vigor which made men free declines too much, or if their ultimate goals remain confused, then a reversion to a world controlled by naked power seems inevitable.

Faith in the progress of free men was a basic tenet of democracy's credo. The founding fathers assumed it, and our rapid rise to prosperity and power seemed to confirm it. That faith did not originate in America; it was as old as the hopes of men. In western Europe it had been voiced for generations by poets, essayists and statesmen. It derived an impelling force from the upward march of the common man, who identified himself with it. New confidence in his capacity to shape his own destiny was the ethos of the army of Cromwell, and reached its peak in ebullience of expression in the words of William Ewart Gladstone. "The world grows better from century to century. Let pessimism be absent from our minds, and let optimism throw its glory over all our souls and all our lives henceforth and ever."

The henceforth was all too brief, for the spirit of those words is more remote from that of our times than the spirit of Gibbon the historian and of the Roman Empire whose decline he recorded. The path illuminated by Emerson and Matthew Arnold, by humanitarianism, science and *laissez faire,* does not appear to many modern Americans to be the highroad along which all men will walk hand in hand toward certain ultimate perfection.

Our grandfathers may have differed a little as to the precise vehicles which would best carry them up the long slope of civilization, but nearly all of them agreed that religion, education and science were among the chief chariots of that hard but sure ascent. Many would have added to these a morality derived from the puritan, a discipline of hard work, an enlightened selfishness in economic expansion, a sincere acceptance of the White Man's Burden, and a judicious mixture of warm ardor and cold baths. It was further assumed by those of Anglo-Saxon origin that they would lead the way.

This confidence that the world was on its way to a well-ordered and sanitary Utopia reached its peak before World War I. That war shook the faith of many Europeans in

human perfectibility. The physical and spiritual foundations of America were less shattered than those of Europe
by wars, hunger and dictators, and many Americans have
kept their faith in the ultimate achievement of an ideal
society, though its realization has grown more remote. That
conviction has not yet been proved mistaken, and without it
earlier Americans would not have bequeathed so good a
life to those who inherited it. Most of the energy and drive
of the western world was derived from it.

But many other Americans have lost that faith, and even
to those who retain it much of its earlier buoyancy has vanished. Man as an individual has been devalued by dictators,
psychologists, mass conformity and the decline of religion.
Scientists and historians in mounting numbers confess that
though they believe in the inevitability of change they are
not certain that change will bring progress. Americans who
still think that perfectibility can be reached now doubt that
it can be attained by the nineteenth-century formula, and
even question the merits of the stern morality, *laissez faire*
and self-discipline on which that formula depended.
Whether this discarding of the firmer virtues means the
softness of decay or the mellow wisdom of maturity remains
to be seen, but the change of attitude is significant. Can
democracy, which was based on that faith; can liberalism,
which led it, retain their vigor and objectives without it?

Liberalism apparently cannot, for it has lost its traditional
aims and incentives. The liberal conviction of human progress could endure only so long as it could demonstrate success,
and a half-century of strife and disillusion has left liberals
with empty hands and confused minds. "Liberalism" in
America today is a far different brand from that of John
Bright and Emerson. It resembles its namesake only in that
both are the middle ground between radicalism and reaction.
The differences between a Gladstone and a Henry Wallace

are profound. They might share a belief in the ultimate perfectibility of man, but their ideas as to how men should be improved, and the part that government should play in that endeavor, would be so disparate as to make common action impossible. The nineteenth-century liberal was devoted primarily to the elevation of the individual; the modern "liberal" to the blanket improvement of society. The difference in philosophy and program is fundamental. The American brought up in the older liberal tradition, and still attached to it, has no place to go in American politics. Its disappearance has left a wide gap between the extremes, which men of all political complexions have rushed to fill.

The earlier liberal recognized the difference between progress and change, and might have sensed in modern "liberals" a confusion between the two. He would have agreed with Ferrero that young societies like America may change very quickly but that such change does not necessarily mean progress—that a gain in size or power is not inevitably a human advance. Americans, however, have taken such gains as comforting signs that cosmic forces are working with them to improve mankind and that God, whose status they have relegated to that of Honorary Chairman of the Board, is on the side of the highest standard of living.

Progress is after all a matter of definition. If a man's standards are such that greater riches or greater power seem to him greater good, then America has made striking progress. It is easy for a man to convince himself that what is nice for him must be good for society—that is a conclusion that motivates most advertising and much social reform. If that be real progress, then its advance in America has been unprecedented. In 1900 there were less than 14,000 automobiles in the United States; in 1950 there were over 44,000,000. This was economic progress, but has it improved our culture? Since 1900 the population of Los Angeles has increased over

74

1900 per cent: opinion would differ as to the value of that achievement. In 1922 the *Saturday Evening Post* sold seven times as many copies per week as it sold in 1902 and got seventy-eight times as much revenue from advertising: during approximately the same period *The Outlook, The World's Work, The Review of Reviews, The Independent, The Dial, The Literary Digest, McClure's* and *Scribner's* magazines died for want of support.

Developments of the means of progress have often been cited as progress itself, and thus obscured the fact that real progress must be in the quality and aims of human life and thought. Accepting acceleration as a sign of elevation, our society also tends to regard past eminence as irrelevant. Gibbon the historian stood before the finest Gothic cathedrals of Europe and reported that he "darted a contemptuous look on the stately monuments of superstition." Complacent modern man could look as small as Gibbon at that moment, from the height of history's cathedrals.

American "progress" is not regarded by the rest of the world with American enthusiasm. Well before he became Secretary of State, John Foster Dulles wrote: "The Communism of Soviet Russia represents today the active, dynamic element and the free world the static, passive element. . . . It would seem that the non-material forces are chiefly serving the opposition." If this statement had not come from a source so unimpeachable, some senator might think it un-American, but until America acts upon the full implications of Mr. Dulles' statement it will not win the unreserved leadership of those elements of humanity that still place some value in spiritual strength.

What has happened to the western world that has robbed it of so much of its dynamism? What is there about America that has kept it from winning to its side, naturally and completely, those who yearn for freedom in Asia and the Near

East? What is the reason why the Voice of America has not been more convincing? Not all the answers reflect on America, for those who hear America's voice from a distance are not always wise enough to detect below the clamor of its strident materialism the undertones of humanity and good will. They too have their limitations in perspective and values. But in the area of humane values and ideals American life and thought are inadequately productive and compelling. Democratic culture is failing democracy.

Why has our culture not kept pace with our material progress? We brought from western Europe a somewhat better balance between material and humane values. The leaders of our early days prized men's spiritual endeavors, from Greece and Palestine through Renaissance and Reformation, and consciously sought to implant those values into their new nation. The men who wrote the Declaration did not declare themselves independent of Plato, Cicero, Erasmus, Luther, Thomas More and Aquinas. They did not intend that their new society should look upon them, as Gibbon looked on Chartres cathedral, with contempt. They assumed that their new republic would continue in the spirit of the Magna Carta and the Glorious Revolution, of Cromwell and Coverdale, of Milton and Shakespeare. Without that assumption their work had no meaning and the structure of their republic no foundations.

But those links with the past were not equally cherished by later Americans busy with the conquest of the west and the pursuit of personal wealth. They developed another philosophy to justify what they wanted and what they were doing. As the attitudes of the uncultivated grew more dominant, our links with the civilization of the past weakened. In our anxiety to be free of anything that could restrain us in the quest for prosperity, we discarded part of our inheritance, but failed to replace the foundations we were sweeping away.

American ideals thus became a mixture of the humane tradition (which had been patrician in spirit) and the materialist revolt (which was popular). There has been and can be no reconciliation between them. To this composite were added new social concepts at variance with those on which the republic was built. Ideas from French revolutionaries, Marxists and German philosophers were cast into the American intellectual cauldron, but these did not blend with the already discordant mixture, and our resultant cultural fare is lumpy, thin and indigestible.

When Darwin and his successors shook the foundations of religious belief and traditional humanism, they accelerated the philosophical disintegration already under way. There have been many other earthquakes. The theory of relativity, for example, was used by many who did not understand it as a justification for substituting flexibility for earlier ethical absolutes. If the length of a meter varies as Fitzgerald says, then why should not every yardstick measuring thought and conduct be shrunk or expanded to suit our practical convenience? Science, with all its virtues, encouraged expediency by weakening traditional codes of human faith and values. Opportunism, materialism and politics have been congenial throughout history, but rarely have they been such powerful partners as in recent American history. Few major political decisions were made during the last two administrations in which expediency was not a determining factor.

In economics, the depression and the New Deal questioned the validity of what had been thought to be economic laws, but established no new absolutes in their places. In education, firm requirements of qualitative accomplishment were replaced by fluid standards that relieved the student from any strain to exceed his estimated mental capacity, no matter how low. School and college grades no longer measure how much a student knows or understands, but only how much more or less he knows or understands than his class-mates. In domestic circles, discipline and obedience to elders became old-fashioned; they were questioned in theory and abandoned in practice. Organized religion has largely departed from its earlier spiritual absolutes and firm disap-provals, in order to make its judgments of human sins more understanding and its creeds more palatable. Honesty is still honored as the best policy, but special exceptions (such as income tax returns, small-type escape clauses in contracts, and time-killing in hours-of-work agreements) are more and more commonly accepted. The Ten Commandments, previ-ously accepted in theory if not in practice, are increasingly challenged in principle. "Why should I honor my father and mother?" Coveting one's neighbor's wife is now repre-hensible only if the husband objects and the court proves alienation of affections. The old adage "Be good and you will be happy" is, with the help of pseudo-psychiatry, being revised to "Be happy and you will be good." These altera-tions have not yet notably changed the ethical code to which Americans outwardly subscribe. But when morals depend on habit rather than conviction, on social custom rather than religious belief, their breakdown is only a matter of time. Much that was narrow and prejudiced has been swept away, but gone too are many of the sanctions by which earlier men had created a civilized society.

Tolerance has been expanded to make a virtue of accept-ing without protest the mediocre and even the mildly un-ethical. We are so eager to be tolerant in all things that we tolerate vulgarity, shoddy thinking, blatant self-seeking and even intolerance with resigned self-applause. It is doubtful that the modern policy of "live and let live" is quite the same thing as tolerance, as Christ (who drove money-changers from the temple) preached it. The word discrimination has been narrowed down to mean only racial intolerance; its earlier meaning of selecting the good and rejecting the bad has been forgotten in practice as well as in definition.

Ethical practice has consequently shared in the specialization that has conquered our professions; it has become local and piecemeal. Different groups in society have differing codes. The business man has one code of ethics, the minister another, the football coach a third, the politician a fourth. The ethic of many labor leaders permits almost anything that will bring wage increases to their unions; the ethic of many publicity men is whatever will make their propaganda, true or not, effective; of most reporters what will get them a good story. Beyond these vocational moralities, some high and some low, there are very few common moral compulsions. As a man moves from group to group within society he adopts, chameleon-like, the ethical color of his surroundings. The moral force of America is homogeneous only in opposition to cruelty, war, injustice, and dishonesty beyond a certain nebulous boundary. We are united chiefly in what we disapprove in other countries. Over every other area of morality our decisions are variable and provisional—solutions of the moment, buttressed with the vague hope that the will of God and the comforts of Mammon can somehow be conveniently merged.

With more faith in law than in themselves, many Americans turn to legislation to make their neighbors moral. De Warville noted this tendency as early as 1791, and commented that laws supply but imperfectly and in a miserable manner the place of morals. Democracy depends upon the ethical character of its citizens or, as Alexander Mackay put it after a visit to America in 1846: "The American Constitution . . . can only suffice a people habitually correct in their actions." If by legislation we ask our government to become our moral mentor we are not solving our problems of behavior but only postponing them. They will come back to us, in augmented form, as government demonstrates its inability to rise higher than its own constituents.

American culture is so new and complicated a phenomenon that no one can yet judge it with omniscience. It is easy to be impressed with its vigor, activity, instinctive friendliness and warmheartedness, and to assume that they make its future secure and its ultimate elevation certain. It is equally easy to find beneath the surface of American society infections that could destroy it.

History and religion both warn that no society can concentrate on things and pleasures without losing its vision of the ends for which men live. We ignore these warnings even as we debate the causes of our increasing national and personal neuroses.

Material acceleration breeds spiritual inertia. No society can speed up so fast in physical things without growing spiritually dizzy, or can so rapidly discard its past without losing its sense of direction and human continuity. The true function of popular sovereignty is to create a society in which men can use their freedom for the enrichment of their lives and spirits, and are encouraged to do so. The purpose of democracy is to bring to all the good and noble things previously available only to the favored few. It cannot do this if it ignores or destroys the noble things before it achieves them. The challenge to American democracy is to demonstrate that it can make its organized magnitude serve the highest, not just the most comforting, purposes of free men. Can it rise above self-indulgence, restrain and direct the uses of the dynamo and the atom, and fulfill its function? A clue to the answer should lie in a consideration of the quality and trends of present American culture, which will be next approached from several angles.

8

The Machine Mind

Anything that's good for General Motors is good for America.—CHARLES E. WILSON.

> *. . . things outward*
> *Do draw their inward quality after them,*
> *To suffer all alike.*
> —Antony and Cleopatra, III, iii.

AMERICA'S DEVELOPMENT of economic power has no parallel in history. That power has enabled the nation to survive waste and mismanagement; to win world wars; to provide its citizens with the highest standard of material living the world has ever known. The magnificence and merits of that achievement are apparent.

Such economic development could not have been accomplished without a cost. The cost is less apparent than the purchase, for the price is paid in intangibles. And even if the cost were visible most Americans might be willing to go on paying it. They find the possession of a new car or deep-freeze and the blessings of financial security more than adequate return for some intangible spiritual and mental losses that may be involved. Let the highbrows worry about them!

So the attractions of wealth and power have led most of us to concentrate upon them to the neglect of comparable achievements in government, education, religion and the arts. The total effect is evident only when the results are cumulated. Material progress is being paid for by distortions in our intellectual values and ways of thought. As our investment capital and income grow, our spiritual capital and income diminish. As we concentrate our minds on economics and technology, we think with less clarity about the functions of democracy, the uses of freedom and the ends of life.

That is, if we think about these things at all. It is easier not to think about them, but to assume that because we are rich, powerful and free we must be intellectually balanced and spiritually sound. Democracy and material wealth have become so closely associated in our minds that many Americans think of popular sovereignty as the cause of national prosperity, and organized labor has made that belief its platform. When politicians, captains of industry and labor leaders extol the blessings of democracy they usually do so in terms of the material advantages it has brought, and Americans have come to think of democracy as a machine existing primarily to raise their standards of living. This concept of democracy stands in contrast with the convictions of Aristotle and Aquinas that the state is an agency of the moral order, and must itself be invested with moral dignity to lead its citizens upward. It is at odds with the conclusion of De Tocqueville that democracy is a means toward the rule of equity and the elevation of the spirit. It does not inspire its citizens to high adventures in idealism or cultivation. Instead of a base camp from which new ascents of human self-realization should begin, our economic security is becoming our final goal.

The American emphasis on material things is so heavy that many men and women have lost interest in any other values, except as they advance material ends or personal pleasure. The average American is a shrewd judge of quality in mechanical products, from motor cars to radios, but his ability to evaluate quality in men and ideas is not equally developed. He is satisfied with no less than the best in airplanes and plumbing but accepts the second-rate in politics and culture. This discrepancy is often excused by the assumption that rising material standards will inevitably raise intellectual and spiritual ones. Material welfare does indeed lay a foundation upon which the mind and spirit can be elevated, but it does not ensure that elevation.

If the drive for technical perfection continues unmitigated by humane culture, it can only end in a completely mechanized society. A mechanized society, to function efficiently, must be a highly regimented society. Such a society is not really free; nor does it encourage humane culture or creative art. Why should it, since they contribute nothing to turning the wheels of further technical progress? Spiritual force and imaginative drive are the only two forms of energy that our engineers cannot harness or measure; it is not surprising that they look at them askance.

This distortion of values was partly a product of industrialization and modern science, but it would not so quickly have conquered the minds of men if industry and science had not been accompanied by the rise to power of the common man. Machine prosperity made that rise inevitable, for industrialization brought demand for labor, and made the workman a valuable commodity in a seller's market which easy transportation made increasingly free. This placed the working class in a strategic position to gain ever higher wages, stronger unions and greater political power.

Great industries produced great cities, and with them an urban society whose mass values now dominate American thought. Recent government reports indicate that some ninety-six million Americans live in cities, and this does not include those who commute from suburbs in which life and thought is essentially urban. Thirty-three millions live in a total area equivalent to a square only fifty-five miles to a side, and the process of urbanization continues. Even fear of atomic bombs has not slowed down urban growth. Between 1940 and 1950 168 American cities added over six million people to their populations, and this is just as though thirty-seven new cities had been built of about the size of Flint, Michigan—except that the actual development made large cities still larger. The nation has arrived at the situation feared most by Jefferson—an urbanized common man whose cultural and ethical development had not kept pace with his rise to political power.

Since large cities are products of mechanical progress, the culture of their urban dwellers is especially adjusted to the machine. City dwellers are less likely than rural residents to own their homes and to have the desire for stability that home ownership brings. There is an impermanence about their thoughts as well as about their lives. Cities are too large to encourage participation in civic affairs by the average citizen, or to develop a sense of personal community responsibility. Children of urban dwellers, though they have advantages rural children lack, do not experience the uncommercial pleasures, the natural disciplines and the rural realities that come naturally with country childhood. Urban masses are more restless, more volatile and more subject to propaganda. Though large cities are centers of culture, the ordinary man or woman may find in them fewer chances for friendship and self-expression than in small towns and villages. In large cities there is less exchange of neighborhood opinion to stimulate thought or curb individual excesses. The late W. N. Guthrie used to say that there was no civilized man or woman in New York City who had not been civilized elsewhere.

The culture of our cities reveals its heterogeneous and uprooted elements. Temporary residents and disoriented citizens dominate our urban populations. Among the latter

are the immigrants and children of immigrants. They settled in our cities, often not from choice, and though they
have contributed variety to urban culture they have added
to its confusion. More than we realize, the mores of south
and east Europe, of Asia and the West Indies, dominate the
culture of our greatest cities. Though some from those areas
have become very distinguished Americans and many have
become valuable ones, their influence as a whole has not
been uplifting.

This was by no means entirely their fault. The ideals they
brought with them to America were distorted or destroyed,
and the substitutes they developed under American pressures
were rarely of the best American quality. Most immigrants
were admitted to America more on their qualifications to
stoke the American machine than their fitness to understand
its ideals or to advance its culture. They became primarily
the under-servants of the nation's economic expansion. Cut
off from the mores of their homelands, they did not find
American society as a whole eager to welcome them to social
equality or to its best cultural fare, or even to explain American ideals intelligibly. Efforts by Americanization committees, schools and churches to make the immigrant an asset
to democratic culture were sporadic and halfhearted, and
only a drop in the bucket compared to the other influences
they experienced. The actual Americanization process was
likely to be a sordid and disillusioning laboratory. Often
forced by lack of funds and language to stay wherever they
landed on American shores, many immigrants were exploited
by industry and racketeers, patronized or socially resented by
Americans of earlier vintages, seduced by crooks and re-
cruiters for vice, and exposed to a tawdry and avaricious
America far different from the noble democracy they had
expected. Small wonder that their reactions were sometimes
cynical and antisocial.

The issue of the immigrant and his children was never maturely faced by the elite and prosperous of society; it was partly ignored and when possible forgotten. Society's treatment of its ten million negroes was even less calculated to make them idealists about American democracy. These "less-chance" citizens and their children comprise at least a third of America's sovereign people. They quickly learned to understand the machine, to utilize its product, to think in its terms. Lacking cultural anchorage this unwelcomed population of America further distorted the balance between mechanics and humane culture.

Our cities also include millions of migrants from rural life in America. They too are disoriented between the values of their country backgrounds and those of the apartment, the skyscraper and the impersonal mass-life of the metropolis. Blindly groping to make the best of two barely reconcilable worlds, they have made the best of neither, and provide no stable cultural nucleus.

But it is primarily the descendants of men and women longer in America and more blessed by its resources that are to blame for the inadequacies of American culture. They are the leading citizens who set our cultural patterns—or failed to do so. Their failure is the least pardonable for their responsibility was the greatest. It was simply a case of too much attention to Mammon, of rendering too much to the Caesar of aggrandizement. The machine provided them with more money, more units of power and more leisure than any society had previously possessed, and thus gave them unparalleled opportunities to attain new heights of intellectual excellence. Instead they used the machine frivolously. They spent more of the money and leisure time it gave them in entertainment than in self-improvement, in collecting than creating, in escapism than in cultural leadership. There were great exceptions, but they were few in number. Those who patronized the arts did so chiefly by purchase, often through professional agents. They were often more interested in displaying their treasures than in understanding them. They wanted to understand; they often wanted to elevate themselves and others—but they were too busy.

It was not only a question of lost opportunity but of abdication of cultural leadership or its subordination to the charms of commerce. The machines which they created to be their servants increasingly dictated (after the manner of modern servants), their masters' way of life. In a modern airship or ocean liner it is easy to see the crew as merely another factor in the ship's mechanism: the human pilot servicing the automatic pilot, the navigator servicing the compass, the engineer servicing the motors. Even their control of where the ship or plane goes is determined by mechanical factors quite beyond the human crew's control. The captain is just as dependent on the plane as the plane is on the captain. It does not take much more imagination to see a factory, and then our whole mechanized world, as one in which human society is simply a function of its own machines, its activities determined by the wheels of production. A machine for men becomes a machine of men. The extent to which the lives of free men are regimented by their own machines is visible when a power shortage leaves millions without heat, light or transportation, or a coal strike in West Virginia throws thousands out of work in Ohio and California.

The machine entered the home like a Greek bearing the gifts of emancipation. Mechanical devices have freed most women from many hours of drudgery, liberated children from daily duties and relieved men from the bondages of stable and furnace. It gave all Americans greater freedom from home responsibility and greater mobility over a wider area.

Instead of using these new freedoms to strengthen and elevate the home, Americans have used them to destroy its spirit. Many homes are little more than service stations. Only economic convenience and the bonds of affection—and sometimes only habit—hold some families together. The modern home usually has the minimum necessary space for food, beds, clothes and bar, and is streamlined for fast service and a quick getaway. The universality of the motor car means that either the entire family takes the road for the evening, or that the domestic circle is nightly broken because either the young or the old are seeking diversion elsewhere. Motion has become a narcotic, almost an intoxicant, to many American families. It does not matter where or how or why they go, so long as they can keep moving. To escape from where they are seems an irresistible urge. Can it be that they are trying to run away from their own spiritual malaise?

The elimination of domestic chores has taken from children the chance to develop a sense of responsibility, of being needed and of sharing. Many children today do little of a responsible and productive nature, at home or outside it. Artificial substitutes for needed help by parents do not achieve their purpose. Children do not like moral gymnasia any better than their parents.

Under these conditions it is not surprising that a recent study of the family reports that ceremony and religion have almost disappeared from the family as a unit. The typical family has become a collection of individuals thrown together by biological and economic circumstances and all too conscious of the fact—each going his or her own way, with separate occupations, separate amusements and separate friends. Most families do not get together; they only live together. They do not communicate ideas, but debate practical immediacies such as who will use the car this evening or what television channel can be agreed upon. Perhaps whatever of value modern parents have to give their children can be imparted in the movie theater or over the telephone or while father is dropping them at school on the way to his office, or elsewhere in physical or mental absentia. Perhaps—but sometime mothers and sparetime fathers have not yet demonstrated that they can give their children the understanding, affection, ideals and discipline they need. And the children have not demonstrated that they possess them.

The influence of the machine is not limited to its physical effects. Its philosophy has permeated the minds of Americans, who try to apply its methods and values to human problems. All technical knowledge is impersonal, and the more our lives are permeated with technical things the more our thinking becomes dehumanized. We tend to think of men and women not as separate, unique individuals, but in terms of collective social welfare, pressure groups, mass reactions, public relations and other fictitious plural entities. When Thomas Aquinas was shown the robot made by Albertus Magnus, he smashed it with his stick. He saw that it symbolized the issue between human values and inhuman mechanics. Because the technical world and the technical mind is impersonal, its attitude toward human culture is passive, neutral, uninterested. Its only ethic is its own efficiency.

It is the logic of the machine that its product is predictable, and if not satisfactory can be made so by improving the machine. This logic is assumed to apply in nonmechanical fields. If government falters, the instinct is to seek the remedy in improved government machinery. If marriage is not happy, then the mechanics of marriage must be faulty: improve the legal relationship, the domestic machinery, the sex technique or the bank account and John and Mary will be congenial again. Or hire an expert mechanic of the mind to adjust the sputtering psyches. If it is then still clear that the dual-controlled marriage vehicle cannot make the grade, then each partner should turn in the other for a new model, getting whatever allowance for the old one the market will bring.

The machine mind has even put its stamp on education, which used to be regarded as a humanizing process. Parents and other institutions of society shared with the school the education and discipline of youth. Now, by the application of the expert-production-line theory, schools and colleges have become specialist machines to which the whole job is delegated. Into them parents hopefully pour their raw material and expect that upon graduation the end product will be fully up to specifications. If it proves not to be, then there must be something wrong with the academic machine or its foremen. In spite of the efforts of the best educators, the school product is tailored to fit commercial demands, and the individual is allowed to forget that he carries within him the whole duty of man and the spark of the divine.

Much of higher education, and especially educational research, is now less concerned with evaluating ideas than with analyzing and measuring talents, and with developing techniques to predict how groups of men will react to some mechanical stimulus. Public relations experts and politicians are interested in automatic mass reactions, and even the average man seeks formulae that will enable him to win friends and influence people by routine procedures. The pursuit of happiness itself becomes mechanical as pseudo-psychological books which offer ten easy rules to personal popularity and achievement become best sellers. The machine is making us believe that there are mechanical means to nonmechanical ends. The individual tends to become merely a statistical unit in a mass reaction—a classified anonymity in a Gallup poll. The rights of the free individual become only whatever rights are left over after the rights of organized producers, organized labor, organized middlemen and organized consumers—all creatures of machine production—have been taken into account. This mental attitude is the enemy of that striving for the best which is the measure of mature civilization; this emphasis on mass reaction is adverse to the development of the individual that was the objective of democracy. The economic man and the civilized man are not synonymous, and the glorification of the former may debase the latter.

There is another way in which the logic of the machine works toward the distortion of human values. To create a demand for their products, manufacturers try to convince every man that his happiness depends upon the constant acquisition of new goods and replacement of earlier models. Advertisements are part of the machine, hitched to its assembly line at the distribution end, to create wants where wants did not exist. Attacking the minds of Americans at all times, from all angles, and often with great psychological skill, advertising inculcates an interesting concept of democratic welfare: that happiness consists of the newest goods for the greatest number; that progress lies in the maximum mechanization of personal life; that democracy is enhanced by the universal possession of uniform goods; that affection is measured by gifts; that social responsibility includes keeping up with one's neighbors in the knowledge and possession of gadgets; that parental duty requires protecting one's children from the sense of inferiority certain to follow the selfish retention of last year's car. Although those who prepare and disseminate this commercial creed have no such conscious motive, the result is to condition the American mind that among the highest virtues are modernity, material possessions and the pursuit of pleasure. Advertising creates a promised land to be gained by alert purchases and prompt installment payments. Americans are drawing near that promised land, without stopping to consider what life will be like in a gadgeted Utopia of streamlined, plasticized beauty and ever self-renewing conformity, in which there need be no human effort except to be worthy of the bright new mechanical perfections.

"What we've got to pinpoint on our radio programs," one sales manager said recently, "is that our sell is not an upper-class quality sell, but more of an intimate, soothing, universal sell."

From the machine-production point of view the perfect man would be a prosperous individual cleansed of all aims above material desires, who would abandon himself without reserve to the collective opinions of majority society and the enticements of advertising. He would be conditioned to forget that a good wine needs no bush, and would believe that if the bush were beautiful the wine must be perfect—until the newer and better wine next year.

The salesman's philosophy has made commercial fantasies of holidays. New ones like Mother's Day are partly created and fully exploited by the minions of the machine. The religious significance of Thanksgiving Day has dwindled before the orgies of special sales and gastronomic self-abuse which the purveyors urge upon a pliant public. The moment Thanksgiving shelves and heads are cleared the Christmas sales begin; the tidal wave of commercialized Christmas cards and "business remembrances" sweeps in. When even the press becomes morally disturbed, its perturbation is news. On New Year's Day 1953 the *Washington Post* said in its leading editorial:

"The American Christmas has become commercialized to an extent that is shocking to many foreigners and that almost transforms it into a national orgy of sentimental materialism. But there also remains the fact that it is not merely the manufacturers and advertisers, but the great part of the American people, who prefer to have it this way." The *Post* made its point well, yet neatly avoided offending its advertisers.

It would not be easy for the American people to overcome the habits of thinking they have derived from the machine. They are unlikely to do so of their own accord. Certainly they would not, even if they could, turn back the wheels of material progress. But the price our minds are paying for the blessings of mechanization is very high, and will become higher as its logic pervades still more deeply the whole ethos of society. Earlier centuries mistook pedantry for erudition; the twentieth century confuses technical knowledge with wisdom.

Can we hope that when American standards of living finally reach some yet unseen high; that when every American is the owner of innumerable perfect machines, our society will then turn its thoughts and values to other than material interests and mechanical thinking? Or is the appetite for luxury unlimited, and does materialism breed still more materialism until all other values are forgotten? Perhaps in time everything that American machines cannot produce will be dropped from American culture.

It is when the machine distorts human values that it ceases to be our servant and becomes our master. Whatever else may be made mechanical, human values cannot. Mechanical techniques, by making society more systematically organic, turn men into cogs. There is irony in the fact that man, in his effort to become only a little lower than the angels, is moving further from the spirit of exaltation that conceived them. As man has reached upward with his hands he has become more earthbound in his mind; as he has become more mobile he has also become more mobilized, and in the technical world mobilization means regimentation.

The machine age is producing a society all dressed up but with no place for the human spirit to go. The members of our society are beautifully organized into a social vehicle to run endless circles in the futile quest for happiness through possessions. Will maturity arrest these adolescent maneuvers, or satiation bring disillusion with material things? How can society gain maturity through immersion in immaturity? The only hope lies in a reaction—in men's ultimate re-discovery that mechanical civilization does not satisfy all the needs of man, but leaves him with an emptiness of spirit. With that realization might come a determination by a few Americans, and then by many, to lift themselves above the mental attitudes of a nation of shoppers.

9

Crowd Culture

We talk about the American Dream, and want to tell the world about the American Dream, but what is that dream, in most cases, but the dream of material things? I sometimes think that the United States, for this reason, is the greatest failure the world has ever seen.—From Give Me Liberty And—, *an unpublished play by* EUGENE O'NEILL, *as reported in* Time *magazine.*

*The Nirvana of the individual is too high a price to pay for a collective Paradise.—*LEARNED HAND.

YOU NEVER had it so good," was the appeal of Mr. Truman to the voters. The slogan was typically his but the argument was not new in American politics. Others before him had found it effective; his predecessor had used it with unprecedented success.

Whatever the truth of the slogan in Mr. Truman's case, its implications are significant. The ancient appeal of bread and circuses has not lost its appeal to the common man; the first thing many men want of their government is personal prosperity. And why should not Americans place a high value on their material standard of living? Health, economic security, sanitation, personal opportunity and national power are all good things. To the average man they also mean a chance to own a home and a car or two, to read books, travel, and send the kids to college. Are these not cultural progress?

The Democratic defeat in 1952 did not mean that the voters had rejected prosperity as their first criterion of good government. If the average man decides that under the Republican administration he is not having it "so good," he will vote it out of office.

There may have been observers in other parts of the world, conscious of its chaos and crises, its spiritual as well as its physical hunger, who viewed the Truman slogan with dismay. Its indication that Americans were preoccupied with their personal welfare did not fortify the hope that America's world leadership would be ethically or culturally elevating. A few Europeans, not superficial or envious observers, may have recalled what earlier visitors from the old world had said of America—observers like Philip Schaff, who in 1855 wrote that "the flourishing commerce and growing wealth of the country involves great danger of bottomless materialism and worldliness." But Europeans could not claim that materialism is a uniquely American phenomenon or that it is solely due to prosperity. Their own democracies, which are certainly not all prosperous, also show signs of overpowering materialism. Perhaps the growth of popular sovereignty, common to all democracies, had something to do with it. So it seemed at least to Justice Gerard of the Court of Appeal in Liége as early as 1908, when he predicted: "What remains of that general culture which has no direct utility . . . is destined to disappear."

Such predictions of cultural decay, for whatever cause, seem absurd to most Americans. They are convinced that society is sound and culturally growing; to predict its decline and then assign the cause to popular sovereignty seems to them almost subversive. Though some of them admit that there is blatant vulgarity in American life, they excuse it as a temporary expression of the healthy vigor of a free society, revelling in its new power to express its own values, certain to be a little crude at first. The logic of these optimists follows a fairly uniform pattern: that the standards of material living and universal education provide a foundation upon which a magnificent new culture will ultimately be erected; that the beginning of a modern American renaissance is already visible in such quantitative facts as the increasing public enjoyment of music, the enormous circulation of books and magazines, the unprecedented number of college students, the large attendance at galleries and museums and the wide interest in the creative arts. Some temporary loss of traditional culture, they argue, is more than redeemed by the fact that a spontaneous new culture is now created and enjoyed by the people—not established for them by an elite and set apart from the common man, who might admire but might not touch.

This logic is supported by emotional convictions Americans have derived from what they were taught, what they feel, and what they see about them. Can any American deny that whatever makes men prosperous makes them good, that whatever makes them healthy makes them wise? Who can breathe the tonic air of America, or stand between its vast horizons, or sense the bigness of its achievements and its plans, or look into the faces of its youth, without joining in the exhilarating certainty that it is indeed the promised land? Only a cynic can remain a doubter amid its boundless energy and popular surge. Its countless neat and modern homes that would have seemed fairy palaces to earlier princes; its schools and factories and playgrounds and libraries; its friendliness, ambition and generosity; its hatred of cruelty and injustice—these arouse a Whitmanesque certainty that in America the spirits as well as the fortunes of men are flowering under freedom.

Perhaps there is more truth in that ebullient confidence than in the sober conclusions derived from looks beneath the surface. Perhaps Americans are right that all they need to do, once the Russian menace is removed, is to continue along the smooth highroad of scientific materialism and popular tastes. Perhaps it is true that in this brave new world of pragmatism there is no Satan except Communism. It may be that the earlier standards by which aristocratic societies measured human progress have no relevance to the march of the people. The new world does indeed bring new values, and what could be more natural and proper that it should first of all bring material comforts and security to those whose ancestors had only the consolations of religion?

For centuries men have argued whether material prosperity is a stimulus to creative genius and true religion, and no one knows the answers. Most great creative art has come from societies in which at least the upper class was flourishing, but a rich elite does not always mean a prosperous people. And the highest philosophy and religious thinking seems to have been born more often in poverty or renunciation than in earthly well-being. Certainly the founder of Christianity did not preach that material wealth encouraged spiritual elevation.

It is probably the atmosphere and values of a society, more than its standard of material living, that lift or degrade its culture and inspire or discourage its artists. The Elizabethan Age in England, the Renaissance in Italy, the rise of the Republic in the Netherlands were all periods when their societies had a vitality of spirit and a clarity of aim—an atmosphere of values—which found dual expression in material prosperity and in cultural achievement. Artists, thinkers, adventurers, artisans, men of commerce and princes all felt the stimulus of that atmosphere and rose to new heights in their respective spheres. Art and thought may not then have flourished because wealth flourished; they may all have been the equal fruits of some deep common inspiration.

The man of rare creative talent is more stimulated by the sense that society values him and his work than by a high standard of living. Conversely, a society that prefers mechanical perfection to great art, or that cannot distinguish the superior from the mediocre in thought and ethics, is a greater enemy to creative genius than poverty can be. Talented scientists are stimulated today by the knowledge that society esteems them, but talented humanists are less creative because they feel less appreciated.

The present spiritual myopia of free society may be only the inattention of its adolescence, which maturity may sharpen to the vision of more elevated values. Those values do exist in contemporary America, for one can find men and women devoted to the finest in art and thought. Their existence is proof that America can value and create well, and gives grounds for hope that under a more mellow social climate their numbers may multiply. But the culture of a society cannot be judged by its minorities or its Sunday behavior alone; its values must be assessed by everything its people create and say and do. A foreign policy and a baseball game are both significant expressions of the nation's culture. The number of its citizens who read comic books may be more revealing than the number who visit art galleries. Is American society as a whole infused with an integrity of values, a loftiness of aim in little as well as big affairs, and a creative urge that is manifested in the striving of countless individuals toward beauty in ideas as well as in things? Do the best of America's intellectual and spiritual products express human understanding and elevation equal to the finest that past civilization has produced? If our culture falls short of this, does the excuse that we are culturally immature still apply, or should we by this time have grown up? To assess democratic culture by such questions compels one to put aside many of the casual optimisms offered in its support, and to set higher standards of humane values in judging creative art, education, letters and our way of life.

The daily interests and pursuits of average Americans do not offer much evidence of loftiness of aim or discrimination of values. Many existing formulae for success and happiness have the simplicity of adolescent games. Even manners and taste glorify the undemanding common denominator. They reveal little more than an energetic unison in the pursuit of the commonplace, and this has been carried so far that the uniformity of the average has achieved an aura of moral superiority over anything that differs from it. To be different, even in one's preferences in entertainment, is to be "queer."

Manners reveal the extent to which a man respects himself and others, and are thus a fair measure of the quality of social values. There is much that is truly democratic and generous in the spirit that motivates American manners. They bespeak a universal friendliness, a directness of effortless simplicity, a confidence that every human being has common ground with every other human, an assumption that the next man is a decent chap until he proves to the contrary. These are the spirit of real democracy, but as expressions of that spirit American manners are often crude. They are depreciated by the tendency to make all social exchange undemanding and ordinary, to presume thoughtlessly upon the feelings or the privacy of others, to disregard reserve or sensitivity, to assume that the other fellow has no right to any standards above those of elementary decencies—and these are the opposite of democracy's respect for the individual. If a foreign visitor conforms and praises, we like him; if he does not, his welcome cools.

American inability or reluctance to rise above the level of the elementary decencies in manners is most clearly shown by the average American attitude toward personal privacy and personal dignity. With the aid of press, radio, advertisers and public relations counsels the personal privacy of any American vanishes whenever he arouses the curiosity of the public. The details of his domestic life and personal habits are invaded and publicized, and he must not only acquiesce to this process but pretend he likes it. Indeed he often seeks it, and intimacies previously reserved for the confession box are now volunteered to nation-wide audiences in the "tell-all" radio programs and confession magazines.

It does not matter much to the public what kind of circumstance has awakened their curiosity or what character of person is its object. We automatically expect that any kind of fame or notoriety will be capitalized into a best-seller or a radio feature. The same season brings the memoirs of a President's wife and of a Polly Adler to the front page; Hemingway crashes in a plane and makes a new fortune by his account of it; James Roosevelt runs for Congress as a reply to charges of marital infidelity; Louella Parsons' literary efforts are consumed with those of Adlai Stevenson; the philosophical opinions of a convicted racketeer are read with as much consideration as those of Albert Schweitzer—and far more widely. In a society where a successful comedian, crooner, boxer or millionaire wins wider adulation than Robert Frost, T. S. Eliot, Toscanini, or Alfred Whitehead, there are few incentives to aspire to top excellence. Success is without real distinction and failure is without dignity.

The familiarity that permeates the manners of America is shown in the public's attitude even toward those citizens it exalts to its highest places. A candidate for public office must assume a pose of genial complacency in order to affirm his democratic spirit; he must not show reserve, subtlety or any sense of superiority. Even the President of the United States, no matter how grave his problems, must be always cheerful in public and jocular with journalists and handshakers. He must produce the vigorous step, the light quip, the easy laugh, the big smile, the "human touch." He might prefer no publicity at all, but this would bring a poor press or even deliberate distortions of his statements as retribution for being "un-cooperative." In fostering informality we have fostered intrusiveness; in renouncing social barriers we have renounced social boundaries; in discarding repressions we have discarded restraint; in eliminating false shame we have almost eliminated shame itself. The American concept of the manners of democracy has forced all Americans to live in glass houses.

The public justifies its manners by the assumption that democracy means personal equality and that personal equality means deference to the least refined. The mass likes informality because it is the great equalizer; it makes few demands and requires no social discipline, no personal effort and no personal achievement to put the lowest on a level with the highest. Anyone can speak of the President as Harry or Ike and few think it either presumptuous or in dubious taste. It is an easy way for the speaker to feel himself on a level with greatness and thus to reassure his own ego. Ceremony of all kinds is in full retreat, and with it the respect for institutions and principles that ceremony was created to emphasize. On those rare occasions when Americans do accept formality, they like the chief actor to violate it by some apparently spontaneous incident to show how "human" he is, and thus assure them that ceremony is only a mutual game. What we fail to realize is that unconventionality demands a finer tact and sensitivity than conventional good form, just as the absence of red and green traffic lights demands more care and skill by the driver.

In private social life informality has paradoxically become conventional, and carelessness of manners has been elevated to a social ritual. The wisecrack, the genial insult, the loud laugh and the peddling of minor emotions are substitutes for conversation. Good taste is no longer an expression of individual value-perceptions. It is determined by external professionals: editors of women's pages and etiquette columns, interior decorators, book clubs and home and fashion magazines. One need only follow their mandates to win acceptance in most circles. The fervor to do whatever is being done has turned personal taste into imitative uniformity largely determined by commercial interests and popular vulgarians.

This kind of social uniformity threatens to create mental uniformity, for those who live in identical houses with identical furnishings, identical manners and identical clothes are in danger of adopting ideas equally identical and ready-made. To progress, free society must encourage variety, and those who take nonconformist positions should not be put on the defensive. Yet those few Americans who make occasional deviations from accepted opinion in even minor matters now feel constrained to be unduly defiant or unnecessarily apologetic. Even the current phrases with which an erring nonconformist explains his social aberration reveal his sense of sin. He "opened his big mouth" or "stuck out his neck" or "talked out of turn" or "went out on a limb." These are not attitudes that encourage or dignify independent opinion. The editors of *Fortune* magazine recently published the results of their own study of American conformity. They found the scene "a little frightening. . . . Conformity, it would appear, is being elevated into something akin to a religion. Perhaps Americans will arrive at an ant society . . . through unbridled desire to get along with one another."

Popular pressures to conform are not toward conformity with exalted models but toward acceptance of the commonplace. A mass society inexperienced in taking the cultural initiative, lacking inherited traditions of taste and the disciplines of humane education, naturally accepts without discrimination whatever pleases it without effort, or whatever is vouched for by the majority. Many of the viands it gorges on are meretricious sweets; others are purveyed by men who find personal profit in vending painless paths to popularity or power. Culture has come to mean the pursuit of devices for self-advancement or self-entertainment, marketed in ten easy lessons, twelve postpaid volumes or eight lectures on Understanding the Universe. That symbol of social sophistication, the Bachelor's degree, sometimes proves to be even cheaper in real value than its cut-rate cost in cerebral effort.

It has become easy for the cultural tenderfoot to believe that culture is purchasable at the box office or the radio shop, the night school or the tourist agency. As a result, a dazed half-attention to the battering adolescence of most commercial entertainment, rapid undigested tourism at home or abroad, and endless reading of the mental regurgitations of others, have become the opiates of the American people. These popular imitative amusements could only satisfy the cultural desires of an undemanding society. With most men and women pathetically eager to like whatever others like, majority taste has become a composite of individual concessions to what each man believes to be the general preference. There could be no more certain road to intellectual poverty and emptiness of spirit, and these are increasingly reflected in modern life and literature.

But there is a deeper reason why popular society accepts the mediocre in preference to reaching for the superior. When the common man rose to power he brought with him a subconscious resentment against the values of those who had dominated him. Envy is a primitive instinct based on a sense of insecurity, and the average man still feels insecure about his cultural judgments and his real intellectual equality. His rise to political sovereignty gave him a chance to express his resentment at his earlier cultural dependence, and his present cultural uncertainty, by belittling earlier culture. Men who are uncomfortable in the presence of superiority bolster their ego by attacking what they have not achieved. Mass assertiveness and opposition to the superior are born of the same emotions, as Ortega implied when he wrote that "the characteristic of the hour is that the commonplace mind, knowing itself to be commonplace, has the assurance to proclaim the rights of the commonplace and impose them wherever it will."

Popular society likes excellence only when it is of a kind that does not disturb its *amour propre*. No society is more given to adulation of those who display superiority in certain popular skills, such as baseball and golf stars and popular entertainers. The abilities of such heroes can readily be measured in terms of home runs, bogies, recordings and dollars, and appreciation of them requires little cerebral effort. That kind of superiority does not trouble a citizen's complacency with his opinions and standards. But if a hero departs from the expected formula his pedestal trembles. Charles Lindbergh was the nation's idol until he felt impelled to depart from the role the public had assigned to him and discuss controversial matters. Now that he has achieved the remarkable *tour de force* of becoming a distinguished writer, he is again a popular hero in a different way. This time he is the man of the hour with the intelligentsia—that same intelligentsia which, while professing its devotion to freedom of speech, was quick to shout "fascist" when it disagreed with Lindbergh's political opinions. Since *The Spirit of St. Louis* does not offend their political party line, they can recognize it as a rare and original book and make much of its author. Einstein was another kind of national hero in a more remote way; almost no one understood him but nearly everyone accepted the experts' verdict that he was a tremendous adventurer on the exalted heights of mathematics. But when he began to express opinions on public issues his admirers diminished. To think independently is to challenge the democratic norm, and "highbrow" and "theorist" are not complimentary terms. "I'd rather be a bonehead than an egghead," is simply the latest slogan to defend the commonplace.

Most Americans want to be cultivated, but only comfortably cultivated. They dabble with the intellectual just enough to avoid being lowbrow and escape being highbrow. Middlebrowism looks like cultivation because it is so clearly superior to vulgarity, but to be satisfied with it is to make the good the enemy of the best. It merely dresses and domesticates the commonplace. Its reaction to real superiority remains a cautious envy.

The cure for envy, as was pointed out in a parable about talents, is for a man to recognize his personal limitations and then gain self-respect by making the best of what he has. The remedy for group envy lies not in trying to make everyone equal by pulling down the best, but in creating a society in which inequality is recognized, and every man who does his particular job well is respected by himself and others. If, on the other hand, society is viewed as a racetrack where every man but the winner loses, or as a platform with only one level to which the inferior must climb up and the superior climb down, mediocrity is inevitable. Democracy as an orderly society need not foster envy or the commonplace; democracy as a chaos of attempted equality is certain to do so, and to bring increasing neuroses to its citizens and itself.

Other things beside the cult of uniformity contribute to the spiritual anemia of democratic society. Man's ultimate goal is to understand the meaning of life and to identify himself with the forces of good. The final measure of his culture is the depth of his spiritual life. For centuries men expressed their religious faith chiefly through the churches, whose variant quality has been a measure of society's fluctuating ideals. The twentieth century decline in the moral authority and spiritual influence of the churches must be recognized. One leading churchman writes of "how small a part the Church has nowadays come to play in changing or preserving the current way of life. . . . such small respect is paid to religious standards of value that most of the younger generation does not even know what those standards are." Millions of Americans do not accept without reservations the creed of any church, and millions more give only physical support to the religion they outwardly profess.

The reasons for this decline have been widely discussed, and most of them will not be repeated here. The authority of organized religion over the masses previously rested on their acceptance of its claim that it could point the way, and even issue passports, to eternal joy and eternal punishment. When the literal existence of Heaven and Hell began to be doubted, or the validity of the church's position as doorman questioned, the church lost its most powerful sanctions. When its monopoly of spiritual wisdom was challenged, its authority declined; when downtrodden masses which had thought religion their only consolation began to experience the more immediate consolations of adequate food, medical care, education and decent homes, the attractions of religion encountered serious rivals. Uncertain of a future world, men concentrate more completely upon the rewards and pleasures of this one. The philosophy of the middle ages stressed the virtues of acceptance in this world and the beauty of the next, but modern science is based upon the perceptions of the human senses, and modern man has been busy in exploiting them here and now, for better and for worse. Competition, not atheism, is the greatest foe of organized religion.

In their efforts to hold their influence over a sensory society, the churches have failed to maintain with uncompromising clarity the spiritual standards of their origins. Some have turned to popular entertainment to lure their constituents at least physically into their houses of worship. Church community centers function with dutiful vigor; coffee is served in the crypt after Communion, and bingo enlivens cathedrals. Particularly in the Protestant churches, sermons have become more mundane and popular, and some churchmen have embarked with more good intent than good judgment upon the controversial political and economic seas of their communities. All these attempts do not appear to have won the public to greater spiritual devotion or deference to organized religion. The causes and remedies of spiritual sloth are too deep to be dealt with by superficial and sometimes cheapening methods.

The inner life of Americans may be less flaccid than it seems, for the strength of the church may no longer be a valid measure of the spiritual depth of individuals. Americans may pursue private lives of the spirit quite apart from organized religion, but that is a hope for which there is little present evidence. Only men and women of unusual strength and devotion can lead deep spiritual lives without guidance and a sense of religious community with others. Conditions of modern life do not make solitary religion easy or even possible, and independent religious effort is likely to be elementary and sporadic.

So far as society is concerned, it gains less from individual religious activity than from organized religion. As a social force, religion must be institutionalized to be effective; upon the rock of personal faith a church must be built. Churches traditionally supported the family and the community in

establishing and enforcing codes of morality and social conduct, and men separately cannot perform this service. Large
numbers of children today consequently undergo no effective
formal religious instruction; they rarely enter a church and
do not think of religion as an important element in their lives,
until some misfortune forces it upon their attention. Whatever loss this may be to religion, it is a profound loss to the
cultural process of society.

With organized religion descending from the heights of
Mount Sinai to the valleys of sociology, with the sanctions of
the next world yielding to the problems and pleasures of this
one, with materialism leading on to hedonism, with democracy and science being exalted into competing faiths, it is
not surprising that the churches are no longer a leading
medium of cultural elevation.

Whatever may be the contribution of other agencies, culture begins at home, and there it has become increasingly the
responsibility of women. Their achievement of political
equality was less revolutionary than their quieter rise to
recognized rule over matters domestic. Most American men
now defer to women in questions involving children, social
relationships, morals and manners. But even this tremendous added responsibility and power has not kept women
from expanding their conquests outside the domestic ménage.
They do most of the spadework in support of community
philanthropies, welfare organizations and civic improvement groups. When, during the war, a handful of business
men gave a few spare hours each week to work in the wards
of hospitals the event was news and the men were regarded
as rare spirits. Women showed great restraint in refraining
from pointing out that they had been doing the same thing
for years. On the national scene, women's organizations do
work more significant than is often realized. Most powerful
of all is the influence women exert on the decisions of men

on all sorts of issues—the men they work with in offices as well as the men they work for at home. In addition to all this activity, few would say that the average woman has restricted her social pleasures to any painful degree.

Perhaps these are reasons why American women have not made a more impressive success of their cultural leadership in the home. The chance to lead a larger life has lured them from the home half-acre their mothers cultivated more intensively. Distant pastures seem to them, as to men, a little greener than the back yard. If the pursuit of pleasure is characteristic of Americans, women have set the pace, and have not discouraged their children from running still faster.

No matter how great may be their energy and ability, it seems doubtful that women can at the same time accept all the opportunities of their new freedoms and still meet all the responsibilities of their enhanced authority at home. They cannot dare do all that doth become a man, and also be the elevating mentors of the family matriarchies. Henry Adams, who insisted that women were abler than men, nevertheless wrote of the American woman of 1903: "She might have her own way, without restraint or limit, but she knew not what to do with herself when free. . . . she had failed even to hold the family together; the family was extinct like chivalry. . . . Whatever [women] were, they were not content."

Just fifty years later, another intellectual, Thornton Wilder, wrote with the daring and relative safety of a bachelor:

"A seismic disturbance has taken place in the home. Within forty years America has ceased to be a patriarchy; it is moving toward a matriarchy. . . . father is no longer held to be, ex officio, wise and unanswerable. The mother has not yet learned the rules of supporting and circumscribing her new authority. Father, mother and children have had daily to improvise their roles. This has led to a constant emotional racket in the air."

Meanwhile the need for America to assume world leadership in human ideals as well as in power puts the issue squarely before the average men who are our popular sovereigns. Dr. Charles Malik, Lebanese Minister to Washington, recently told Americans what the rest of the free world wants from them:

"Can the United States develop a type of man who sums up in his culture such a quality of understanding, of humility, of humor, of moral stature, of strength and resourcefulness of mind, of pregnant ideas, of universal friendship and love as to enable him, by the sheer weight of his being, to overcome the disadvantages of mass and discontinuity? It has not yet dawned on America how much is required of it to develop this kind of humanity."

That is a high ideal of democratic leadership. The reality is often something quite different. Commenting on the Czech statesman Beneš, Nicholas Roosevelt wrote: "He lacked the egotism, the vigorous personality, the dramatic powers and the ruthlessness which seem standard equipment for men of the leader type." Even in the most admired statesmen of this century, those qualities have been more in evidence than the ones Dr. Malik calls for. Most of modern democracy's leaders have displayed little of the moral force of a Washington or the humility and spiritual depth of a Lincoln.

Even the greatest optimist would admit that America has a long way to go to fill in quantity Dr. Malik's qualitative prescription. The pessimist would say that it cannot be done short of the millennium. But when the American people see an objective clearly and desire it strongly there has been no limit to their capacity to attain it. But to produce leaders who advance humane values, a society must esteem those values, and to do that wholeheartedly America would have to change its cultural trends. The phrases of Mr. Wilder can be borrowed to describe the current state of American society, which suffers from its own emotional rackets. The American people is relatively inexperienced in its full sovereignty and has not yet discovered the rules of supporting and circumscribing its authority in politics and in culture. Its members are improvising their roles. Unfortunately a social order of consistent values cannot be created or maintained by improvisation. Nor can it be advanced by popular sovereigns in whose daily lives the inflation of material interests debases the cultural currency. The most frightening pages in history are those which reveal how easily a cultivated society can be turned into a desert of the human spirit.

10

Custodians of Culture

*In truth, everything is against distinction in America,
and against the sense of elevation to be gained through
admiring and respecting it.*
                              —MATTHEW ARNOLD,
                              Civilization in the United States.

THOUGH DEMOCRATIC culture is determined by
the people, they cannot *en masse* originate it. The popular majority accepts or rejects what is placed before it. Its
decisions are innumerable and often unconscious, for national culture is the product of all men's personal reactions
to the ideas embodied in books, music, comic strips, inven-
tions, manners, conversations and prejudices. Democratic
culture is always flexible because always under revaluation,
but if its standards of judgment themselves become fluid,
culture moves toward chaos.

Those who create new ideas for submission to the popular jury are relatively small in number. Without their creative stimulus democratic society would be intellectually
inert, and their vigor and quality is therefore essential to
culture. But even the finest creative spirits cannot elevate
culture unless they are esteemed by the average man, whose
values and standards therefore become the crucial issue.
The average American has not warmly accepted the highest
flights of the creative mind. He prefers intellectual showmen
or barkers who do not tax his brain or imagination too heav-

ily, who only mildly titivate his convictions, who seem to value what he values. The danger of following such hucksters of culture is that they are more likely to accustom men to the commonplace than to lead them to the creative.

The popularity of the easy adaptation has discouraged exceptional minds from elevated leadership of art and thought. Some of them, reacting against the popular showman, go to the other extreme and devitalize creative art by making it, and its criticism, too cerebral and too consciously highbrow. Others turn in discouragement from the humanistic arts to less frustrating careers; still others merely lead democratic culture from the rear. As these groups abdicate effective cultural leadership, it is left in the hands of a larger group of educated but not creative or highly intellectual men and women. These are the middlebrows, who to varying degrees support the interests of the more creative spirits. It is they who read the better books and magazines, see and hear the plays and music and art that democracy produces; support its orchestras, galleries and colleges. They form the medium in which ideas are tested and thought distilled. Since their limitations will be pointed out, it should be made clear that they are nevertheless the backbone of what is best in American culture, as well as of its philanthropies and politics.

Educated in the tradition of the liberal arts, with some sense of the perspective of history and the slow, fragile accumulation of humanism through the centuries, these men and women incline toward the preservation of continuity and quality in culture. But their education in the basic humanities has usually been fragmentary or superficial; it has left them with qualified enthusiasm for the arts, with little confidence in their own cultural judgments, and with understanding hardly adequate to make them skilled and ardent defenders of humanism. Anxious to keep up with the ideas and fashions of their times, they have tried to appreciate and patronize the new, from progressive education to Dali, while retaining the best of the old. They are not sure—as who can be?—what is valid and what is pseudo in modern art and thought, what is permanent and what is outworn in our cultural heritage. They have found their faith in the traditional canons shaken but their life with the new pragmatism and impressionism uncomfortable. Eager to be tolerant, they have acted as though tolerance meant the discard of convictions, and have often absorbed without discrimination. Thus relatively chartless in the troubled seas of thought and taste, they have failed to influence the rest of society in any definite direction, and are more the victims than the arbiters of cultural confusion.

The more conservative members of this confused intelligentsia feel out of the main stream of democratic taste. Their sense of remoteness from popular values and new thought has made them less vigorous in asserting their own standards. They privately deplore society's discard of traditional disciplines and standards in taste, manners and education, but have not loudly protested. Although these rear guard defenders of the older humanism have contributed some balance between the excesses of extreme modernism and Grand Rapids imitations of the traditional, they have done little to clarify the issues and less to settle them.

Their ineffectiveness has been somewhat offset and somewhat augmented by a smaller and more vociferous group of cultural arbiters who flourished or fulminated in the Twenties and Thirties. This little company of men and women were more confident in their judgments, more professional in their attitudes, and more ready to defy popular standards. They wrote, edited or reviewed serious books; created or criticized modern art; taught or researched in humanities or social sciences; headed consciously intellectual discussion groups, and were rarely at a loss for an opinion. Often widely traveled and with some claims to sophistication, they made it their business to be informed, to pronounce, to convince, to debunk. Confident of their qualifications, they announced their minority dicta with defensive belligerency. They were never a close or organized coterie, for they were unified only by their opinionated eloquence and their spiritual *malaise.*

Between the two world wars many of the men and women of this pursuasion were to varying degrees alien to the American culture of their time. Only a few were expatriates in the physical sense; most of them lived and worked hard in an America with whose popular values they were somewhat at odds. The extremists among them saw, or said they saw, very little in America that they could approve, but the majority were only casual and sporadic in wearing the mantles of their disillusionment. If they embarked on cultural crusades they did so more to escape from what they disliked than to pursue some clearly conceived and greatly coveted goal. Generally naïve in politics and economics, they were especially vulnerable to the Marxist appeal, and some even flirted with communism in their salad days. The artists among them, less emancipated than they thought, conceived art as a temple and artists as a priesthood of the anointed and dedicated, who should be above an interest in the mundane problems of the rest of society. If society turned its back on them, they turned their backs on society and lost some power to interpret to their contemporaries. Their firm opposition to materialism, provinciality and any repressions of self-expression was a valuable contribution to America, but their virtues were largely negative. They stimulated society but did not offer it a new foundation on which it could build those finer relations between men, and between men and God, that they talked about so eloquently. From their artistic efforts came a little, like Scott Fitzgerald's best, that was somewhat important, and much that was not. Their greatest influence lay in the atmosphere they created and the attitudes they made popular among the intelligentsia. Though these men and women are no longer as prominent or as intransigent as they were, their influences and their imitators endure. The cynicisms they fostered, the frustrations they featured and the wastelands they proclaimed left their marks on current arts and letters.

Meanwhile the popular culture of America has fallen almost entirely under the influence of those who make a business of the management and purveying of art, music, letters and thought. Their commercial atmosphere and attitudes predominate. The creative arts have always had their patrons and entrepreneurs, but rarely have the economic aspects of all art creation so affected its nature and its values. What is encouraged, exhibited, published, accepted and played is largely determined by dealers, publishers, producers, professional critics and directors of art galleries, and this is especially true of the new arts of cinema, radio, television and commercial illustration. Such entrepreneurs are the props of contemporary American culture, but they exact from creative artists all the compromises that follow an interest that puts marketability first and artistic integrity second. Since what these purveyors offer makes the bulk of what society sees and hears, the popular jury is largely limited to choices between the commonplace and the fashionably extreme.

Commercial custodianship of democratic culture has as its first axiom that what is popular must be good. If one declines to accept that criterion, then there is no way to judge the quality of current art and literature except by traditional standards, for no others have been developed. To apply the traditional canons to some modern works of art, by men who have sincerely abjured the older standards, may be to do them some injustice. They could claim that since historical criteria were developed in aristocratic societies, or previous to modern psychology and nuclear fission, they have no validity as measures of modern democratic art. Others could argue that a wide spread of popular self-expression is more important to democracy than the quality of its product; that perhaps upon the foundations of the popular culture now in formulation qualitative skyscrapers of democratic culture will eventually arise. Such arguments center about the conviction that the twentieth century is so different from all preceding ones that none of the earlier rules apply.

All civilization before 1900 cannot be so summarily discarded, nor can one reasonably claim that a present culture is good on the purely presumptive grounds that a finer culture may evolve from it. Thus far in the experience of society, the creation of a few great works of art, rather than the proliferation of inferior ones, has been the mark of a high culture. Perhaps in a democratic society this will not prove true: no one can yet be sure whether the human spirit will flower best in a society watered from the top, or left to spontaneous and uncultivated germination at the grass roots. But it would seem that even a popular society must have before it a few peaks of superb excellence, in works of art as in men, to which it can raise admiring eyes. If the highest standards are once forgotten or denied, they can be regained only with the greatest difficulty. The mean level of the ocean would be lower if it had no high tides.

The development of creative art in America is impressive if measured only in quantitative terms. Music, for example, is said to be undergoing a renascence. Through concerts, radios and recordings more Americans than ever before are regular listeners to music of some sort; there is a mounting number of American composers and performers of high quality, and symphony orchestras have multiplied in number and attendance. Youth has discarded the notion that to make or enjoy music is effeminate and has become its most enthusiastic audience. Most impressive of all is the *élan* which enlivens the popular musical world.

The analysis of this situation which follows is not intended to belittle the important progress in music. Its motive is to suggest that quantitative measures of cultural advances cannot be taken at their face value, and that when other relevant matters are considered the case for American cultural elevation is not as reassuring as it appears. This applies to all creative arts; music is selected as the chief example because it has the strongest case; in music if anywhere artistic creation and appreciation are in the ascendant in America. The analysis that follows does not conclude the contrary, but offers reasons why we should not accept too readily the optimistic verdicts which purely quantitative estimates bring.

Since music is a qualitative art, it cannot be judged solely in numbers of participants and patrons, or volume of production. Qualitative measurements are difficult to make, but such as can be made are less encouraging. In musical composition a few Americans have attained excellence and more show great promise, but the nation has not yet produced a composer of the very first order. In musical performance America excels, but only with the help of musicians born or trained abroad. Of its reported three hundred symphony orchestras, though several are among the best in the world, the quality of most is distinctly inferior. The excellence and popularity of the best American music schools, such as Juilliard and Eastman, may work wonders in another generation, but at present where qualitative superiority exists it is not wholly native.

Music is primarily an active and not a listening art. A truly musical nation makes as well as hears music. But the vast majority of American musical enthusiasts are quiescent listeners. Music in America, whether classical or popular, is made by a relatively small number of musicians, mostly professional. This statement may be denied by those who will remind us that there are cases of spontaneous amateur orchestras of good quality in some communities. Query, however, fails to produce any considerable list of these, and most musical groups of this type have been short-lived. The fact that a few such spontaneous groups are the subject of so much enthusiastic comment indicates how rare they are in proportion to the total population.

There are also large numbers of high school orchestras and bands, but to think they represent wholly spontaneous and continuing enthusiasm for music by promising youthful musicians is to reveal a lack of familiarity with the procedures and motivations in our high schools. High school orchestras and bands are from the point of view of most high school youth extra-curricular activities which bring local esteem to participants and credit to the school. Playing a horn or a violin may bring less kudos than scoring a touchdown or leading in the school play, but it has comparable social values. It is naïve to think that pressure from parents and school to display the musical ability so painfully gained by private lessons plays no part in the making of school orchestras. The attractions of uniforms, travel, free entrance to athletic games, and the atmosphere of being in an admired activity certainly supplement the pleasure of making music. Only if the young people who make up these musical units continue through their later years to pursue and improve their musical performance do they demonstrate any real devotion to music. Few of them do so, and most of those who make professions of music do so at the level of dance orchestras and local radio stations and music teaching in schools.

No matter who defines what is good music, he would agree that in America one hears much that is less than good. According to *Billboard* magazine, Americans buy five or six "popular" records for every "classical" one, and *Billboard's* definition of classical music includes some that not all cultivated Americans would call first-rate. And it is not simply a question of what recordings are bought, but of what recordings are most listened to, and heard with understanding and appreciation. For any American who chooses to listen to the best—no matter how "best" may be defined—how many other Americans are listening at that moment to something quite different from that best? There are some clues to the answer. Juke box listeners comprise a cross section of popular society, and their offerings are limited to popular songs and dance and jazz music by whatever is its latest name. Radio disk jockeys make it their business to provide what their listeners want, and they provide a similar limited diet.

Even if one accepted the purely quantitative expansion of music as evidence of cultural progress, the case would not be as convincing as it seems. There are more Americans, with more money, more leisure, better transportation and more chances to hear music, at home or elsewhere, than ever before. If musical consumption is adjusted to these factors, the present musical renascence might prove to be only one more phenomenon of mass production and consumer acceptance. These factors are stated, not to deny the impressive popularity and vitality of music in America, but because to ignore them is to be led into unjustified complacency.

If literature is taken as a measure of the nation's cultural progress the same doubts occur. Much excellent reading matter is being produced and its readers are numerous and increasing, but its volume and their numbers are tiny islands in a sea of producer and consumer inferiority. Never have so many words been printed and spoken that are not worth reading and hearing. Reading can be a road to Parnassus or it can be escapism from the realities and duties of life, a drug to the spirit, a narcotic to the mind. Just as radio has its listless listeners, literature has its millions who read avidly but read little that taxes their minds. These consumers of literary pablum seem to be a product of popular culture in all free countries. Dennis W. Brogan recently wrote, "Progress has been the same in Britain as in the United States; as mere literacy has spread, so apparently have taste, decency and the power of reflection diminished." And the newsstands of the Continent bear this out.

One example of this passive literary omnivorousness is the capsule reading that is the steady diet of many literate Americans. Most magazine articles are in themselves compressions, but readers of the digests, news letters and tabloids get summaries of summaries. The questions asked about literature in some radio quizzes indicate a literary cultivation of about eighth-grade level. Judged by the paper novels, magazines and soap operas, millions of Americans are living in a dream world of romantic or lurid unreality, of crude stimulation of the senses in a fictional society with no subtleties and no inhibitions. The significance lies not only in the apparent wish to escape reality, but in what the consumers choose to escape into—adolescent sentimentality or physical unrestraint. Germans were doing this kind of reading before World War II. Tarzan was their favorite, but he is mild compared to the heroes of our drug store libraries.

Even the quantitative case for American literary culture is weaker than it seems. The Institute of Public Opinion reports that "fewer people buy and read books in this nation than in any other modern democracy." The average Briton, the report continues, reads three times as many books as the average American. Denmark, with four million people, has over half as many book stores as the United States; Sweden with a population of seven million has nearly as many public libraries as America. Gallup's sampling of American college graduates indicated that only one in six had done any serious reading in the previous six months; that only one in two could name a single recent title he really wanted to read; that out of every twenty college graduates eight could name the author of *Vanity Fair* and one knew who wrote *Tom Jones*.

If the arts reveal cultural decay in democratic countries, it is partly because free society has lost some of the compelling guidance of spiritual aims. The secular forces of modern education, democracy and science have been thought sufficient to elevate our culture. But all men have felt the need for guidance and inspiration beyond their own limited powers, and from the beginnings of civilization have turned to some supernatural mentor to direct their efforts and ease their fears and bondages. Since many free men have discarded established religion as a compelling personal guide, they have tried to fill the spiritual vacancy by deifying the new benevolent forces of science and democracy, forgetting that there are spiritual principles greater than either of them. Science brings knowledge and power, but it cannot create ideals or human wisdom. Democracy has brought freedom and wealth, but an inflated concept of its capacity to elevate has confused the American mind. Society has demanded of them a divinity they do not possess.

In a great culture its creative arts reflect the nobility of its visions; in a flaccid culture they betray the poverty of its ideals. Music, painting, letters, philosophy and religion express the basic values which inspire and unify a people. If society is not infused with high values, its artists are not likely to express them. The middle ages derived their unity from a common faith in a divine power that stood superior to the evidence and understanding of the human senses. Chartres and Milan cathedrals were expressions of that faith. Gradually this concept changed. Men came to believe that the true realities and values could be found through what their own senses could come to perceive, or their scientists could wrest from the secrets of nature. Though this was not necessarily the conviction of the great philosophers and scientists it became the premise of the majority, and the Age of Reason developed into the Age of the Senses. The perceptions of the senses alone have not yet brought humanity a coherent unity, and the incoherence of much modern art and literature derives from the incoherence of man's sensory perceptions. Signs of reactions from this purely sensory approach are visible in the work of some ultra-modern artists and writers, but in their revolt they do not often escape from the sensate, but merely represent it in some new, bizarre interpretation. They do not intelligibly point the way to a unity beyond it. Such art is fundamentally more immature than sophisticated, more negative than idealistic.

No custodians of modern culture have maintained higher standards of professional excellence than our best men of science, or have seen more clearly its limitations as well as its promise. They recognize that the function of science is to pursue factual truth in those physical areas which can properly be detached from human values. They know that the strength of the scientific method lies in confining itself to areas in which facts are verifiable and actions predictable, and that those areas cannot include ones in which men's emotions and ideals are involved. But not all scientists see themselves and their work with such perspective and modesty. A mounting number of our lesser scientific minds justify E. M. Forster's reference to "the confident scientist, who patronizes the past, over-simplifies the present, and envisages a future in which his leadership will be accepted." Science can help men to understand the universe and themselves, but before the mysteries of human faith and imagination it stands mute.

Popular society, impressed with the spectacular successes and promises of science, has set no limits to its potentialities. It thinks it sees in science the providential force which will achieve human perfection—the perfection that traditional religion and Gladstonian optimism failed to produce. Faith in science has contributed to the diminution of the individual man as an inviolate agent of the divine. The new broom of scientific detachment has been used to sweep away much debris of the past, but also much that earlier men found valuable and inspiring, and much that the best scientists have never renounced. As a result many men have come to accept human life as Hardy described it in *The Dynasts:*

". . . peoples, distressed by events they did not cause, are seen writhing, heaving, and vibrating in their various cities and nationalities . . . like animalcula in tepid pools . . . eternal artistries in Circumstance."

And to conclude with Robert Bridges that the Twentieth Century is "the almighty cosmic will fidgeting in a trap."

Those who see life thus, and also lack full understanding of science, try to use its methods in fields where its validity is doubtful or absurd. The method of science is the accumulation of all facts conceivably relevant to the problem; the analysis of those facts until some hypothesis can tentatively be drawn; and then, with complete detachment, the testing of that hypothesis until it can be proven true or false. When this method is applied to areas where human relationships and emotions are factors, it loses validity. In human problems it is difficult to determine what are facts and what are shades or aspects of truth which may be equally important. Since everything that has touched life is relevant to the human problem, very little can be eliminated. Controlled experiments are not possible. The student of humanity must make, as the chemist should not, allowances for the motives, emotions and personalities of men; the doctor must consider, as the nuclear physicist does not, the personal psychology of his patient. The economist, after all his statistics have been analyzed and his "scientific" laws applied, must still allow for sudden consumer boredom with a previously popular product, or the effects on American trade of a religious war among the Arabs, or the plain pig-headedness of human beings unwilling to do what is obviously in their own economic interests.

Enthusiastic imitators of scientific methods in human areas have encouraged an over-rating of facts. "Nothing in education," wrote Henry Adams, "is so astonishing as the amount of ignorance it accumulates in the form of inert facts. . . . All opinion founded on fact must be error, because the facts can never be complete and their relations must always be infinite." Facts are the basic material of intellectual endeavor, but they have value only when given significance through interpretation. The historian must select from all the events of history those which his trained judgment and vision tell him are significant. Indeed, he must look beyond the recorded facts into the minds of men, and perceive correctly the thoughts and emotions that determined the inner decisions that made the facts. That Caesar crossed the Rubicon is less important than why he crossed it. The facts of history and the arts cannot be evaluated objectively because they were not made objectively, and scientific objectivity puts aside the most valuable tool of the humanist—his subjective interpretations. The current admiration of scientific objectivity has made us subjects of the arid reign of undigested data.

Just as the success of science has led to exaggerated expectations and misuse, so the prosperity of democracy has brought inflated ideas of its capacities. Science and democracy are limited means to limited ends, not panaceas for all the troubles of mankind. Science is a way of coming to know the physical world; democracy is a technique and an attitude for the mastery of the arts of human association. There is nothing in either of them which justifies their elevation to the role of agent of the divine. Both require long training in self-discipline and understanding before they can be made to operate successfully. To attempt to use the scientific method where it does not apply, or to operate democracy among people where its ends and methods are misunderstood is to court intellectual triviality and political disaster.

No greater disservice has been done science and democracy than to distort them from means to ends; to assign them power and functions beyond their mundane uses; to harden them into dogmatism and conformity. Yet some of their worshipers rival those of the old Church in insisting upon their own infallibility, and even assert their personal capacity to distinguish between apostates and true believers in democracy and science. They sometimes pursue their self-appointed investigations of the purity of a man's democratic faith, or of his scientific creed, in the spirit of earlier inquisitions. The culture of free men cannot rise to its highest levels until they liberate themselves from the delusions that science and democracy are magic formulae.

These discussions have disclosed characteristics of some of the custodians of popular culture who have put their stamp on America's literary and artistic product. If one knew nothing of the arts and letters of contemporary America, what would one expect to find in them as a result of these characteristics? Let us imagine a scholar familiar with all human history except that of America. The little that he knows of us is derived from a pained but tolerant reading of the preceding chapters. We have persuaded him, in a rare moment of scholarly abandon, to offer his deductions about a culture he has never known. Those deductions follow.

Each reader can judge for himself their resemblance to reality.

This mythical person might conclude that American emphasis on the factual would have produced a wealth of documented and orderly analyses of contemporary society and its many activities, more didactic than philosophical in content and more prolix than distinguished in style. For the same reason he would expect that some of the best American writing would be in biography and history, and that its greatest strength would lie in the relation of contemporary events to one another. He would predict that the weakest points in such books would be their over-concern with the immediate, and the inadequacy of their relation to the past and to the universal. He would suspect that American social scientists would deal less well with the spiritual forces that move men and determine events than with the outward and immediate causes. Would there be a danger, he might wonder, that such great concern with the factual and the social would minimize or neglect the importance of the individual and his personal visions, and lead art to the service of social ideals and even propaganda, as he understood had happened in more extreme ways in Hitler's art and Stalin's science?

He would not expect to find that the creative artists of so economic and factual a people would offer many soaring flights of pure imagination or religious exaltation. He would not hope to find poetry a best seller, or great beauty in most existing verse, but he would be a little surprised that a nation so socially conscious and nationalistic had not produced more serious attempts at the epic or patriotic verse. He would be prepared to search in vain for fantasy as a notable quality in literature, delicacy in the plastic arts, or universality in painting and music. What fantasy existed, he might guess, would be flights based on the factual conquests of science and mechanics.

Impressed by the strong commercial interest of American society, this imaginary speculator might be led to ask several questions. Might not writers and artists, whose recognition and livelihood depended on pleasing not the cultivated few but the less cultivated many, be greatly tempted to produce whatever would appeal to popular taste? Would not the cultural elevation of the Middlebrow and isolation of the Highbrow mean that even serious thought and art were adulterated to please the almost-intellectual, and become chic but not urbane, stimulating but not profound, elegant but not beautiful? Since public taste has firm conventions, might not the need of artists and writers to please that taste mean excessive conformity to standard patterns of plot, sentiment and idiom—the happy ending, for example? If an artist or novelist had produced one commercial success, would he not be almost forced by his commercial sponsors as well as his admirers to forego attempts at new thought or expression and to repeat the successful pattern, too often and too quickly to realize his best talent? Would not the pressures of success make artists unwilling to wait out their literary pregnancies and acquiescent to premature deliveries? And, trivial though it might seem until its effects were fully measured, might not the need of an artist to keep his name favorably before the public lead to the distraction of his creative capacity and the dilution of his artistic integrity by lecture tours, public appearances, literary cocktail parties, press interviews, radio and television engagements, pot-boilers and ready opinions on all subjects?

This detached scholar would draw several inferences as to the effect of the discard of traditional standards on the nation's creative art. He would deduce with pleasure that there would be a wide variety of artistic experimentation and a generous eclecticism among the consumers, but he might also predict less happily that an artistic jargon and a confusion of values would result. He would wonder whether modern artists had developed and made clear—or were even seriously trying to do so—new criteria to replace the older ones they were impatiently discarding. Could it be that there was no artistic standard except what the consumer was thought to like? If that were the case, would not the arts become a chaos of competing groups, each loudly shouting its own excellence, while the public deferred to the most vociferous or the most touted? Would not the only question in the layman's mind, as he stood before a new work of art, be whether he ought to swoon or scorn?

If popular acceptance were the measure of all arts and letters, then the artist or writer could avoid the rigorous disciplines previously thought essential to fine creation, and could conceal his technical inadequacy or his imaginative poverty by aggressive adventures into the bizarre, the lurid or the pretentiously unintelligible. Was there any danger that all who would not accept the new artistic fashions would be accused of Philistinism, with all the intolerance of which the accusers themselves had once complained? All this might have the merit of stimulating experimentation, free self-expression and new thought, but it seemed likely to produce a consuming public more omnivorous and docile than discriminating. Meanwhile, what would happen to the traditional ideas of art, which, though they might seem narrow to the new spirits, have developed over the centuries some virtues worth preserving? Under a social system in which pressures to conformity were so strong, it seemed to our imaginary scholar that even the patterns of experimentation and revolt would solidify into their own conventions. Had he been familiar with modern American architecture, he might have used it as an example of what he meant, pointing out that the new functional was already congealing into patterns which made it no longer adventurously functional but the victim of its own dogmatisms.

But to this mythical critic, envisaging a culture by hearsay, those doubts would seem minor compared to what he would fear to find in the American arts as a result of its perplexities and inanitions of the spirit. Much of its literature might be Laocoön-like wrestlings with the frustrations of man in relation to society, of society in relation to an insecure world, and of both in relation to their spiritual hunger. Fiction might be less a story than an unprofessional case-book of the emotional misadventures of individuals caught between a mechanistic society and their own egos, or between the resolved will of traditional morality and the created pleasure of recognized biology. Literature as a whole would probably prove to be better at delineating characters and situations than in relating them to universal man or the will of God. Because American society had apparently forgotten that man's only significance is in relation to the past and the future of human development, many artists might have become the victims of self-isolation from any sense of their personal link with men that were and men that would be. Their work might therefore consist only of their own subjective reactions, without identifying themselves with the similar thoughts and feelings of humanity of past and future —forgetting that art is not only an end in itself but also a means of addressing humanity. Since (our Olympian friend would continue) the only memorable works of art are those that reveal some facet of a man's relation to the world and the spirit beyond himself, would not this cultural narcissism make the creative efforts of most modern Americans, and consequently their national culture, less enduring?

Much of all democratic art might therefore become marked with the malaise of a generation that had discarded its past and doubted its future. It would reflect a society which, though outwardly vigorous, wasted its energy in the pursuit of trivia, and revealed beneath its surface a profound spiritual ignorance. Even our recreations, so largely purchased, might come to deny the derivation of the word, and instead of being re-creative be merely a jaded escapism from the tensions that the rest of our lives create.

The final conclusion our detached ruminator would feel forced to reach would depress him most. He would deduce that our creative art would reveal in our society a lack of spontaneity and joyousness in contrast with the appearance of ebullience created by its activity. Perhaps as a result of the passion for painless culture, the public would end in taking its art like pills, for quick relief, or like Coca-Cola, for sweet effervescence. If later, he found that books with formulas to bring peace of mind and popular treatises on Understanding Oneself were best sellers, he would not be surprised. If he noticed how much of pictorial art for entertainment purposes in cinema, television and advertisements, consisted of puppets imitating humans, or animals imitating humans, or humanizations of comic strip figures that were themselves distortions of humans, he might be thrown into a whole new area of speculation about American escapes from reality. But his greatest wonder would be that a people blessed with such freedom and opportunity should be satisfied with a culture that gives them so little joy and beauty.

11

The Laboratory of Democracy

You can convince the wise; you can convince with more difficulty the ignorant; but the half-educated you can never convince.

—East Indian saying

THE EDUCATION of princes has always been a serious business. When the people themselves are the princes, their education to meet their sovereign responsibilities is equally necessary and even more difficult. A single prince can be educated under controlled conditions, but the countless youth of democracy cannot be insulated from all the variant influences about them. Instead of a few special tutors all society is their instructor. The community is their laboratory, its mores their manual, its opinions their text. Schools and colleges are merely middlemen, dispensing to youth certain facts and values accumulated and approved by society. No discussion of education for democracy is realistic if it considers only school and college; it must include what youth gets from all its off-campus instruction.

Every society, primitive or mature, has indoctrinated its young, from the initiation rites of South Sea tribes to the youth movement of Hitler. Most societies have done so in conscious support of their own perpetuation, and their indoctrination has been one of stern responsibility and discipline to that end. Democracy, whose future, more than any other government, hangs upon the responsibility and

133

discipline of all its citizens, has been remarkably indifferent to the conscious and strictly-organized social conditioning essential to its own self-perpetuation. It has conditioned, but not according to any consistent plan toward social elevation. It has made much of education within the schools, but very little of education outside them. Its methods are haphazard and its indoctrination piecemeal. And in the American democracy, this conditioning takes place in a society with little homogeneous culture and considerable philosophical confusion.

Early schools and monasteries were established in deliberate isolation from street corner and market place, so that the influences on youth could be controlled. Religion and mental training were by policy combined, not by policy separated. American educational establishments, though sometimes with thicker walls and higher towers than medieval monasteries, are far more vulnerable to outside influences. Mundane society has invaded the campus and the curriculum; all barriers to the free exposure of youth have been removed, and academic education no longer inculcates principles professedly superior to those of the popular society about it. The atmosphere of the school or college campus is almost as worldly as that of the market place. The conflicts to which modern youth is exposed are no longer between academic and worldly ideals, but between the variant values of a confused and mixed society, casually presented by press, radio, night club, playground, cinema and corner store.

In older nations the standards and patterns of culture were set by some kind of an aristocracy, but when America essayed democratic government it embarked upon cultural as well as political unknowns. In the earlier stages of their democracy the people deferred to the leadership of the more cultivated, but when they discarded an elite they made themselves the arbiters of national culture. Their culture determines the quality and objectives of its youth, which absorbs it by daily osmosis. Because practical learning is what society values most they value it too; because it is immediately applicable to their lives it seems to them more valid than book learning. What the young man learns about self-discipline on the football field, about observation from his guide on a camping trip, about economics from a summer job, about manners from country club dances, about morals from his fraternity brothers—these things seem real and are remembered. He accepts the lessons of daily experience more readily than the precepts of the classroom. This has doubtless been true of all youth in all ages, but it is a fact that our system of preparing for citizenship seems largely to have ignored. The man who said that if he could determine the songs of a nation he cared not who controlled its politics must have had premonitions of the cultural power of radio and juke box. School is progressively losing the competition for the minds and mores of youth.

This is partly because academic instruction still attempts to impart theory, whereas youth prefers practice, and does not coordinate the two. Stop a young man on a college campus, where his mind works automatically in academic patterns, and ask him what he knows of the structure of society, or of labor union economics, or of applied psychology. If he has not taken courses by those titles he will probably reply that he knows nothing. But ask him on the street, where his mental pattern has returned to normal, about the local negro problem, or the strike at the local factory, or how best to appeal to his uncle for the loan of a car, and he will offer ready and confident opinions on these applied aspects of those same academic titles. He sees formal education as a series of courses unrelated to one another or to him. Only his vocational studies that serve visible ends seem real to him.

Educators have wrestled with this problem, but in the end most of them have accepted popular standards, and have given up trying to point out that academic ideals should be different from those of the market place, and not less respected. Our schools and colleges are consequently more successful in servicing society than in improving it.

There is a considerable difference between Jefferson's dream of national public education and its current reality, yet the average American assumes that Jefferson's plan has been magnificently realized. Outwardly it appears so. The physical plants of some large city high schools exceed in size and comfort those of certain ancient and distinguished European universities. The number and size of America's educational institutions, the tremendous sums provided for their erection and support, the almost universal ability to read and write, the high quality of our best scholarship and research—these seem to represent the near fulfillment of the democratic dream.

But since education depends on more than desks and dollars, making all Americans good citizens and gentlemen of cultivation (even the phrase is old-fashioned) has proved a far more complicated task than Jefferson could foresee. The tremendous growth of the nation required an expansion of schools and colleges unprecedented in history, with teachers in number and quality beyond the capacity of society to supply. Immigrants with variant cultures diminished national unity and added to the problems of mass education. Industrialism created huge urban centers with their slums, their insecurities, their racial and societal isolations, their conflicts and their Babel of tongues. A nation of men and women eager to better their economic positions insisted that academic education give them vocational training at no matter what cost to humane learning—and American business was by no means averse. Two world wars first upset the schools and then flooded them; the classical studies almost died out and the liberal arts went into full retreat. What the average schoolboy learns and fails to learn would dismay Jefferson and surprise many of today's older generation.

A few citizens recognize these developments and are deeply disturbed by them. Others are aware of them but think them exaggerated or only temporary. The majority of Americans are too impressed by the outward signs of educational progress to give the matter serious thought. They are fooled by good enamel over cheap wood, and rest their confidence on the high level of American literacy. The ability to read is a useful tool, but it can be turned to quite other purposes than the service of the cultural angels. The printed word may put a man on the road to wisdom or it may make him twice as vulnerable to mediocrity or mental confusion. It exposes him to every influence words can bring to bear, but it does not of itself arm him with the ability to discriminate between them. The reading matter most easily available to him is as likely to degrade his taste as to elevate it, to strengthen his prejudices as to remove them. The solution is obviously not to remove the tool of literacy but to teach those who possess it what to do with it. The Germans have given the world two painful demonstrations that a nation can be highly literate without being wise or humane.

Over-impressed with this educational machinery, the average American assumes that it can, with a few adjustments and additions, assure an improved and even more marketable product. Because education costs more every year, he accepts the claims of the professional educationists that it is getting better, and concludes that since it was never so unanimously patronized by youth it must be on the right track.

It has not occurred to him that not all educationists are really educated, that curricular change does not always mean progress, or that the academic tinkerings and additions of recent years may not have removed the old problems but added new ones. So far as many school men and school boards are concerned, if the customers seem satisfied, why worry? But, most of all, the complacency of the average citizen about his schools ignores the fact that even if they became uniformly excellent the values they imparted would then be in conflict with the values of the society around them. Schools could not produce ideal citizens so long as the social laboratory of youth's daily experience retained its present values and standards.

The average citizen is complacent partly because he is not familiar with the general level of political literacy in the United States. Formal schooling is no final test of political wisdom, but it is certainly a relevant one. In terms of exposure to academic training the American people is not as thoroughly educated as is often assumed. According to the 1940 census, of 73,691,000 Americans then over twenty-five years of age, six out of ten had no schooling beyond the eighth grade. This limited education is matched by limited interest in national affairs. In 1940, 49,000,000 out of 95,000,000 eligible voters went to the polls to elect a president, and since 1912 the average of eligible voters who cast ballots in national elections has been about fifty per cent. According to a 1949 survey headed by an editor of the *New York Times,* three out of ten voters were unaware of almost every event in American foreign affairs; only one out of every four could be considered reasonably well informed, and even they had large areas of ignorance. One month after Congress authorized the Marshall Plan, following several months of public discussion, only fourteen out of every hundred voters could give a reasonably correct statement of the Plan's purpose.

The general complacency toward national education is also derived from ignorance about the schools of the nation as a whole. The average citizen may know something of his local school, or of the private school his child attends, but his knowledge rarely goes beyond his immediate personal connection. He does not realize that most of the post-war expansion in schools is vocational, or in social and athletic facilities or physical plant; that these have become so important that the humanistic studies are minimized or crowded out; and that the public schools are largely under the influence of a new type of teacher called an educationist, whose values and objectives are quite different from those of the teachers of his time. No one has told him that some of the best college admission officers privately believe that today's average high school graduate is less well prepared to do the essential work of a good college than the average graduate of thirty years ago. He does not hear college faculties complain that the freshman year must be spent in teaching students how to study and in giving them facts and attitudes they should have learned in school. He does not know that the intellectual knowledge and maturity of the average American schoolboy of sixteen is well below that of the product of the same age of most western European countries. He has not read the conclusion of Alfred North Whitehead: "In the schools of antiquity, philosophers aspired to teach wisdom; in modern colleges our humbler aim is to teach subjects. The drop from the divine wisdom, which was the goal of the ancients, to text-book knowledge of subjects which is achieved by moderns, marks an educational failure." No one has called his attention to the statement of the recent National Educational Commission: "The American people as a whole . . . has never achieved a clear and adequate comprehension of the nature of education in relation to democracy or of the nature of democracy in relation to education."

National satisfaction with the school system has often been tempered with reservations, however, when citizens have considered its individual products for their own purposes. Business men have frequently complained that graduates show little desire to accept responsibility, to plug away at a subordinate assignment, or to realize that the faithful performance of routine is essential to advancement to more exalted work. Military men have reported that young Americans can be made into superb soldiers, but only after they have first undergone an unusually long and expensive period of hardening of the mind as well as the body, since when they start their military training both are surprisingly soft. President Eisenhower has recently supported this conclusion by stressing the need of giving young men a better understanding of democracy. Chairmen of better citizenship committees have expressed concern over youth's indifference to the duties that go with the freedoms of democracy. Parents have regretted that their children lack steady habits, moral convictions or respect for tradition and experience. Deans of colleges have confessed that only a few of their students can be counted on for responsible leadership in student self-government. Medical examiners find an alarmingly high percentage of American young men to be victims of physical or psychological ailments that make them fail to meet normal military standards. Social workers report that youth resents the normal restraints of society, and quote figures on the high percentage of young men and women in the criminal class.

These criticisms are sometimes lightly disposed of by remarking that every generation has deplored the irresponsibility of the next, but criticism of modern youth even comes from some of its own members. The opinion of a young American Rhodes Scholar, written for publication in 1953, may be more convincing. He wrote of his generation that it has "scrambled for security" and has been "pressured into liking the things it ought to like"; that it is "uninteresting . . . its dreams are small, and it will get what it wants . . . too many young writers have read too little . . . we have lost even the continuity of traditions."

There are no signs that youth will fail to defend democracy, for when faced with the issue they have always met it magnificently. They are also at heart far more democratic than their parents, and almost completely free of race or religious discrimination. The danger is that they will accept democracy on too easy terms. If they do, it will be less their fault than that of the society that determined their values. If youth fails to elevate democracy it will be partly because society concentrated upon making its young people competent and adaptable, and ignored other virtues.

Democracy has been content to reproduce itself and its standards. Yet it cannot afford to be static in its levels of human excellence; it must always be moving consciously toward self-improvement, infused with a spirit of lifting the average to the superior. It cannot safely preach complacency, conformity or equalitarianism.

The self-satisfied concept of a static democracy has impaired its education. Schoolmen have concentrated so heavily on one essential of democracy—equal opportunity for all —that they have neglected the second essential—exceptional opportunity and recognition for the exceptional. More time and money is spent in bolstering the academically feeble than in developing the strong. Many of those whose native endowments qualify them for leadership do not receive the inspiration or training to realize their promise, and society does little to urge the schools to supply it. At best these exceptional students are directed into extreme specialization, where they become remote from social and civic experiences and, like Dr. Oppenheimer, naïve about them. Youth as a whole does not emerge from our schools and colleges with high civic understanding or motivation, with respect for quality in culture or even the ability to perceive it.

Most men active in education and civic affairs would deny that they neglect the full development of the specially talented. "Education for leadership" is a popular phrase. Principals would protest that they are in constant search for rare excellence in their pupils, and are prepared to give it special opportunity within the limit of budget and teacher capacities —but those are tight limits. Business men would say that their selection, training and promotion of employees are based on the demonstrated capacities of the individual and that the best are given special treatment. Some civic leaders would explain that they are always on the alert for able young men to take their places, and ready to make them understudies in civic affairs. All of these statements are reasonably correct, if one accepts limited definitions of talent and leadership.

The mass education system of most public schools is ill-adapted to the identification and special treatment of highly talented pupils. Teachers and principals, often limited in their own perceptions and values, use criteria at variance with those of Jefferson, Horace Mann or Henry Adams. They assume that high grades are the sure measure of intellectual potential, that an aggressive but pleasing personality is a sign of potential leadership, that docile conformity or ambitious industry means fine character. Success in the development of an *aristoi* of talent and virtue is also handicapped by the facts that not all teachers believe in it, and that many who do fear that the community would regard special attention to talent as undemocratic.

The programs of business for encouraging and advancing the exceptional are often very good within their limits, but they are arbitrarily restricted by defining talent in terms of potential business success. The qualities that make a good business man are not identical with those that make a great statesman or leader of culture. American business has notably broadened its concept of industrial leadership, but the personnel criteria and training that serve its private ends are naturally not aimed at public service. A training program which makes excellent sales or production executives should not be expected to develop men for distinguished service in public affairs. Business could not reasonably be asked to subordinate its own functions to those of civic or cultural education. In justice to its endeavors it should be added that the present attitude of most labor unions toward employment and promotion does not aid business in the advancement of men on grounds of talent alone. The labor unions' own training for leadership also has distinct merits, but general cultivation and detached social perspective are not notable among them. Yet even wise industrial leadership, to say nothing of political and cultural leadership, requires humane wisdom. On this issue Judge Learned Hand recently wrote:

"I am arguing that an education which includes 'the humanities' is essential to political leadership. By 'humanities' I mean especially history but close beside history and of almost, if not quite, equal importance are letters, poetry, philosophy, the plastic arts, and music. . . . These are fitted to admonish us how . . . wisdom is to be gained only when we stand on the shoulders of those who have gone before."

The studies Judge Hand advocates are declining in educational institutions and in popular esteem. The proportion of college students enrolling in courses in the humanities, social studies and liberal arts (except as they are directed toward strictly vocational uses) has been in steady decrease, and the trend would be even more striking if colleges did not list as liberal arts students many whose interests and preparation are primarily scientific and professional. The humane studies have lost standing as well as numbers. Their teachers often lack the vigor and confidence that attracts students and holds them, and they have not shown imagination in making their subject matter seem more valid to modern youth. The relatively small budgets and salaries of departments of study in the humanities are a clue to their academic standing. Meanwhile the home, the church and the market place are also minimizing humane cultivation and attitudes and even respect for them.

The effect of all this on the new generations is hard to estimate. Generalizations are often unfair to the individual and may be only half-truths. But if one were to characterize post-war school and college graduates *en masse* one would have to say that they seem surprisingly cautious in decisions and action on the major questions that trouble society. Perhaps this is because they realize that they have tremendous gaps in what used to be thought to be the knowledge fundamental to an educated man. Others are unaware of this lack; still others aware but unconcerned. The attitudes of most post-war youth are tentative and provisional except on issues affecting their vocational futures. They do not seek new worlds to conquer, or burn with a reformer's zeal. They are acquiescent to current mores unless driven to revolt by some personal frustration, and then are apt to react with emotional naïveté. Often they display, for external appearances at least, a lethargy of spirit depressing to their elders, who know how much they will need all the spiritual energy they can summon up.

Who is to blame for these cultural limitations and spiritual quiescences? Modern youth is the product of years in which wars and cold wars attacked idealism and faith, in which depressions made men put economic security first, in which education minimized the values of humanism, in which parents were baffled and organized religion failed to inspire.

If youth is immersed in the immediacies and pleasures of the day it is only following the examples of its parents— parents who feel frustrated that they have so little to give their children that their children seem to value.

Modern youth does not shrink from intellectual ardors when the objective is concrete, highly desired and reasonably attainable, but if the end is remote or intangible they waste little energy in its pursuit. They are "practical." Applied science and business practice rank high in society's esteem and bring concrete rewards; youth pursues what society values. Since no generation was ever offered such a flood of commercialized and effortless pleasures, young people, like their parents, absorb them omnivorously. Perhaps these habits reflect a sense that cultural intangibles and long-term rewards are futile endeavors until mankind decides whether its future is to be peace, continued purgatory or destruction.

American youth is conventionally thought to be ebulliently vigorous, especially in its games. The reputation has outlived the fact. Except when there is some compelling reward or some powerful pressures, most American young men are physically relatively passive. In spite of headline interest in college football, basketball and baseball, many young men never attempt them and only the handful who play such games well play them regularly after the school years. Scores of college men take no regular exercise beyond the minimum college requirement, which is often boastfully evaded, except when the stage is well set and equipment and conditions are of the best. Hardly anyone skis except at ski resorts, runs except on a cinder track, swims except at a standard pool or bathing beach, or walks except for lack of transportation.

The small percentage of young men who do play strenuous games regularly takes them with semiprofessional seriousness, urged as well as aided by professional coaches, free equipment and travel, and generous headlines. Many play less for pleasure than for kudos or profit in some form. Such young men either become professional athletes or immerse themselves in business lives often more sedentary than the average. Many other college men limit their college athletics to cheering sections and vicarious expertness as to the batting averages, scoring records and knockouts achieved by others, and by placing weekly bets on teams they never see.

Television and radio have helped passive sportsmen to separate themselves still further from active participation. Twenty years ago educators were deploring "spectator sports" where thousands sit and watch a few heroes perfom. Today the spectator can lie on a couch at home beside a television set, and the sportsman who braves the elements in the Yankee Stadium or Yale Bowl is a comparatively rugged outdoor specimen. Montgomery Ward, which formerly supplied plows to farmers and hunting boots to the hardy, now offers "spectator sports shoes for men" in its famous catalogue. "Television sports slippers" should be forthcoming.

The relevant point is not whether competitive games have physical or moral value, or whether the discipline of physical fitness has merit for youth, or even whether exercise is fun. The point is that even in sports the great majority of young people are relatively passive except where there is some tangible and compelling reward for activity. The point is that they take even their games vicariously. The results are that the atmosphere of most active games, particularly in colleges and universities, is almost as specialized and commercial as are the economic aspects of American life. The laboratory of the varsity field no longer encourages spontaneity, initiative or even pleasure; it is a serious and organized business and youth helps make it so.

In spite of weakened bastions, schools and colleges remain the greatest fortresses of humanism. They could be the centers of elevating influences toward spiritual values. The quality and attitudes of those who teach are therefore vastly important to society. Yet intellectuals of the non-academic world, and even many in university faculties, are unfamiliar with the institutions and programs that form the minds of most of the nation's teachers. They do not know what is taught in teachers' colleges, at what level, or by what kind of person. They rarely know at first hand the personal quality and philosophy of high school principals and their staffs— what is their concept of education and democracy; what kind of pressures and prejudices influence them from within and without; what forces have conditioned them. Nor have our creative writers and critics, personally interested in the future of American literature, investigated the present literary curriculum and standards of the schools, considered the qualifications of those who teach youth to write and read, or found out what proportion of the total school population is ever seriously exposed to any traditional literature.

Those academic well-heads of culture and democracy are largely in the hands of the culturally limited, the intellectually second-rate, and professional educationists quite unlike Bliss Perry, William Graham Sumner or other past and present humanistic teachers. Many present instructors are neither advocates nor examples of humane culture.

Meanwhile that other great educator of youth, the off-campus laboratory of democracy, pursues its random course without standards, objectives or an awareness of its own responsibility. The human product of these combined forces is fortuitous, its political quality dubious, its cultural quality low, its spiritual quality neglected. Democracy has demanded from the products of its own human laboratories little excellence save vocational excellence. That is all it is getting.

Good grain can come only from cultivated earth. To be facile without depth; to have knowledge rather than ideas;

to have facts without opinions and opinions without facts; to have principles without thought and thought without principles—these are to carry the imprimatur not of culture but of sophisticated barbarism. We opposed that barbarism in two world wars, and oppose it again, yet we are in danger of producing by carelessness what others produce by design. Can a democratic society which leaves to chance and misguidance the quality and ideals of its future citizens hope to remain strong and dedicated?

12

The Classroom of Democracy

America's vast system of tax-supported secondary education is not fulfilling its duty to the mind. . . . Its greatest weakness has come from playing down academic scholarship . . . in favor of universality at a level of intellectual aptitudes adjusted to the common denominator. . . . To deny the esteem and prestige which nature attaches to excellence is no service to democracy.
—PRESIDENT HAROLD W. DODDS *of Princeton*

THE PREVIOUS chapter has considered our schools and colleges only as contributors to the training of men for civic duties. Academic institutions have other cultural functions to be considered here.

Whatever their failings, the schools of America have made great contributions to the general welfare of democratic society. They have given the nation almost universal literacy and a broad minimum level of general culture. They have instilled the principles of democracy as their teachers have understood them, and have been a powerful influence toward ending religious, racial and class prejudice. The school system has been the nation's best melting pot, and has helped to preserve and improve social order. It has contributed greatly to the ideals and health of the community, supported the dignity of man by treating its pupils with more personal respect than any comparable educational system, and developed a national physical plant and organization adequate to the needs of the nation. It has imparted some facts which have proved useful to its students, some attitudes which have elevated their thinking, and some mental and moral discipline invaluable to them and to society.

Our schools have done all this with teachers and officers poorly paid and often poorly qualified. They have done all this without the close support of many community leaders best qualified to help them. They have survived, not without scars, the demands and diversions of wars and witch hunts, the reduction of operating budgets, the decline of fixed social and ethical standards, and the innumerable daily pressures from the well-meaning, the self-interested and the ignorant.

Nevertheless the achievement has been inadequate to the need. In his analysis of The American Mind, Henry Steele Commager, the Columbia University historian, wrote in 1952:

"Americans had experimented with mass education on a scale never heretofore attempted and its college and university population was as large as that of the rest of the world combined, but it was not certain that Americans as a whole were either better informed or more intelligent than their nineteenth century forebears; neither the level of the press nor the standards of literature had improved noticeably, while the popular culture represented by the lyceum or the Chautauqua of earlier generations was more sophisticated than that represented by the radio. . . . That the American mind was more mature in the mid-twentieth than in the mid-nineteenth or even the mid-eighteenth century was by no means clear."

Whatever is valid in that comment derives partly from uncertainty and disagreement as to what the primary task of free public education should be. To its founders its purpose was primarily to qualify the common man to meet his responsibilities to democracy and to God. Later Americans added further objectives, often without considering whether their pursuit impaired the original aims. They asked their schools to prepare students for specific earning occupations; to adjust their psyches and personalities; to remedy their personal defects; to instruct them in social behavior and the arts of courtship and marriage; to provide medical care and health instruction; to teach adults as well as children; to find reasons why no child should be dropped from school; and to accomplish all this with a minimum of pain, effort and expense to child, parents and community. Combined, these activities make a chaos of educational ideals and an assignment impossible of qualitative achievement. American education has magnified its way-stations and diminished its destination.

School men as a whole have evaded facing these conflicts by devoting themselves to eclectic expansion and technical methodology. But progress in techniques has not brought clarity of aim. Is the first need of the nation vocational competence, or rationalists who will judge situations on their immediate merits, or humanists who maintain inherited culture, or specialist experts in every possible field, or men of uniform character and personality? What end or ends of education are appropriate to the new citizen—woman? It is ironic that with these questions unanswered the schools have developed extensive systems of guidance, without being sure where guidance should lead or whether the guides know the way. Most educational guidance consists of elaborate signposts along an unfinished road.

These diversities of aim have been magnified by the diversity of pupils and by the problems of mass education which the schools have had to face. Only one who has taught can appreciate the full differences in methods and values between instructing a class of a dozen interested and equally competent pupils, and trying to teach fifty or two hundred with variant abilities, backgrounds and degrees of interest. The first can be an exchange of opinion, a sympathetic drawing out and stimulating of individual minds; the second must be didactic, wholesale, impersonal, superficial. "When, according to our custom, a teacher undertakes, in one and the same lesson, to train many minds differing so largely in kind and capacity, it is no wonder if, in a whole multitude of children, he can hardly come upon two or three who can reap any real fruit from their teaching." Though that could have been the plaint of a frustrated teacher in a modern public school, it was written by Montaigne in 1580, yet the fault of his time has not been corrected but magnified after nearly four hundred years.

It seems reasonable to many members of American society to ask its schools to do for its children everything that their parents do not. It should not seem reasonable to educators. They should have opposed with organized vigor the disintegration of educational unity and disciplines by the indiscriminate expansion of the numbers, content and aims of education. They have not as a profession opposed it. There are exceptions, for American education has been served by many men and women with high intellectual ideals and courage, and much that is finest in America is due to what they gave their pupils. But not all teachers who have ideals have courage, and not all who have courage have vision, or that special talent necessary to influence public opinion. A few educators firmly opposed the triviality and mediocrity to which popular ideas were sure to lead, but their reservations were submerged by greater numbers of educationists and principals with inferior standards and vision, who had the advantage of claiming that what they did was "democratic." So the majority embarked with enthusiasm upon glorification of the average, deference to the vocational and emphasis on the peripheral. They did not realize, or else did not care, that this would mean the undermining of humanistic disciplines and regard for high excellence. They encouraged the public to believe that American education was sound in principle and practice, and that its perfection depended only on the generous provision of further funds. Much of the public accepts this comfortable assurance and this pleasing deference to its own ideas. Educators, who should have claimed the authority in their profession that doctors and lawyers assert in theirs, weakened by their acquiescence their own prestige and self-respect.

Conditioned by mechanical civilization to assume that anything can be produced efficiently if the right formula can be found, Americans began to wonder why, after all these years, its public schools had not found a single recipe which would produce more satisfactory results. This led them to follow the most glib and promising of educationists into rosy paths of pseudo-education, without stopping to consider that education could not be quick or painless without being meretricious, that it could not be standardized without being mediocre, that results that were immediately useful might also prove shallow. Men deep in the thought patterns of commercial practice subconsciously viewed education as a commodity, purchased by specified time and money, to be delivered in a streamlined, standardized, guaranteed package on the agreed date. Many educators, while protesting this attitude, did their best to gratify it. So vocationalism begins to turn education into an insurance policy or an investment plan.

The course of compromise is revealed in a single example from higher education. When, during the last war, college and professional school courses were shortened and accelerated to meet military needs, few educators believed that the quality of the results would be up to normal standards; that a college which had done a fair educational job with six hundred students could suddenly do an equally good job with two thousand on shortened courses. The experiences of the war justified their reservations, but when veterans with public funds swamped the colleges with applications most educators changed their minds. They did not openly say: "This we must do for public service or public relations, though it will further lower our standards in ways from which we may never recover." Instead they reached the popular and lucrative rationalization that standards would not be lowered, and some even convinced themselves of its truth. What had first and rightly been a necessary temporary evil (from the point of view of good education, at least) now became a permanent good, and they excused as public service the watering down of higher education that almost invariably resulted—not lowered by the quality of the veterans, in most cases, but by the quality of the expanded teaching staffs and the makeshift classes. It was a question how many veterans got their (or the taxpayers') money's worth. Sometimes this inflation of the academic currency was not the work of faculties but of presidents, trustees, regents and governors. It was certainly another step toward the triumph of the pseudo-intellectual from which society will be long in recovering.

This educational dilution would not have been so generally applauded if education had previously made clear to itself and society what its proper aims should be. Instead, the catalogues of many colleges had for decades professed an equal devotion to the mental discipline, general cultivation, vocational competence, character, religion, health, morals and manners of all their students. Even professors within the individual colleges differed as to which of these ends should constitute their primary objective in teaching. Those variant aims naturally led the public to wonder whether the educators knew what they were doing, and to make forceful suggestions of their own.

What education was really trying to do was to please the public without excessive compromise of the humanist ideal, but the habit of compromise increasingly obscured the ideal. Spokesmen of liberal arts tried to maintain that waning philosophy, but found it did not pay in terms of students, bequests or popular support. Administrators and educationists were in the ascendant. The phrase "the educated man" came to mean a man with a degree—any kind of a degree. Education means something quite different to a city superintendent of public schools and to a professor of history or philosophy, yet students prepared for college under one concept are expected to thrive under the other. The differences in outlook are too fundamental to be happily reconciled. Until one ideal or the other is generally accepted as the primary objective of democratic higher education, confusion and inefficiency will continue. If the pseudo-psychological and vocational concept dominates, American culture will become wholly trivial and materialistic.

It is difficult to escape the conclusion that American education is not elevating popular society but merely informing it, and that it is not preserving humane culture but diluting it. Each year American schools and colleges graduate thousands of men and women vocationally competent, mentally alert, socially confident, orally fluent, intellectually broadminded and superficially sophisticated. But those who look beneath the surface of these attractive graduates find limitations in mental self-discipline, humane values, firm ethical concepts, historical perspective, qualitative standards and depth and accuracy of knowledge. In the effort to "prepare young people for the life they will enter" education and society are giving them little vision beyond it. Modern young Americans are probably the first victims of an educational system whose objective is not to make them wise but to make them adaptable. The minds of youth are being directed toward acceptance of the commonplace and the intellectually superficial except, sometimes, in the disciplines of their chosen professions. Often the results are cultural ignorance and spiritual lassitude.

The standards and ideals of education can rise little higher than the quality and vision of its teachers. There has been a great shortage in the number of teachers needed for our expanded schools and colleges, but a greater deficiency in their average personal distinction of mind and spirit. Even in teaching purely technical skills, the personal qualities of the instructor are of considerable importance, but in teaching the liberal arts they are crucial, for the instructor must illustrate in himself something of the values he teaches. It is impossible to measure personal quality and general cultivation by any rule of thumb, but both are presumably enhanced by education. Some clue to the cultural level of our teachers is provided by the extent of their own schooling. In 1920 there were some 600,000 teachers in American schools. Of these about twenty-five per cent had not completed more than two years of high school education, about five per cent had had no schooling beyond the eighth grade, and only twenty per cent had had the equivalent of more than two years in any kind of college, studying any kind of courses. Half of the total had taught less than four years.

The men and women those teachers were instructing in 1920 are now determining the ideals and conduct of the nation, writing its books, running its government and bringing up its children. The academic training of the average teacher of 1954 is more extensive, but it falls short in amount, in content and in quality of what is needed. Those who elect to teach do not in general represent the best minds or the most energetic spirits of their generation. Between the best thinking in America and most teaching in America lies a gulf too wide for easy communication.

The past twenty years have brought into classrooms and laboratories a large number of instructors in technical and vocational subjects. These may be extremely competent in their specialties, but most of them have cultural backgrounds even more limited than those of other teachers. Yet next to instructors in athletics, they have the greatest personal influence on students of any category of teachers. Most of them instill into their pupils the narrowness of their own cultural limitations; some even belittle the humanism and general cultivation they do not themselves possess. Since a good many of them make their teaching supplementary to outside activities, or a temporary profession, they have little interest in education. Their contribution outside the specific technique they teach is at best negative.

Some states have attempted by legislation to elevate the personal quality and vision of school teachers by requiring them to take "in-service" courses. This is an incomplete remedy. Minds are rarely broadened or ideals lifted by exposure to a few scattered courses, often methodological, in summer and night schools, particularly if they are reluctantly endured to meet a legal requirement. Good universities which offer such courses are often privately dismayed at the low standards they feel they have to allow. Another kind of well-meant but futile educational legislation is provided in the code of statutes of the State of Indiana:

"It shall be the duty of each and every teacher who is employed to give instruction in the regular courses of the first twelve grades of any public, private, parochial or denominational school in the State of Indiana to so arrange and present his or her instruction as to give special emphasis to common honesty, morality, courtesy, obedience to law, respect for the national flag, the Constitution of the United States and the Constitution of the State of Indiana, respect for the parents and the home, the dignity and necessity of honest labor, and other lessons of a steadying influence which tend to promote and develop an upright and desirable citizenry."

Legislative optimism could go no further.

One measure of what the public most esteems in education is what it aids through gifts and subsidies. Of the $350,000,-000 thus allocated to colleges and universities for special purposes during the academic year 1952–53, according to the *New York Times,* about ninety per cent was for research in the physical and biological sciences. Such imbalance of support is partly due to defense research, but the abnormality has already been of long duration and has profoundly distorted the values of higher education. The great private gifts to colleges and universities over recent decades have been mostly toward medical care, scientific research, business education, dormitories, gymnasia and student social centers. Little support has come from any source to history, philosophy, religion, literature and the fine arts. As support goes, so go salaries, academic prestige and student interest.

Mounting specialization has been the phenomenon of modern education. It has been encouraged by public interest and gifts, by the vocational urge, and by the professions. In professional education some specialization is inevitable, but it has become so extreme that leaders of the professions are themselves disturbed. The ideal of the early scientists was to reach an understanding of the unity in the physical world. The effect of modern science is to divide knowledge into isolated cubicles and thus obscure its unity. In medical education more and more departments are being established both by addition and division, thus creating specialties within specialties and making co-ordinated instruction ever more difficult. In the words of Dean George Packer Berry of the Harvard Medical School, "the rapidly growing mass of scientific knowledge is simply engulfing (the medical student's) educational opportunity" and "the pressure is becoming intolerable." He urged the profession "to regard with a critical eye the mounting tendency to impose specialization."

In the physical sciences specialization of programs and attitudes, even at an early undergraduate level, has gone so far that it disturbs some of the scientific specialists. In engineering, where early specialization has long been deplored by educators, it has reached the point where the undergraduate is usually unable and sometimes unwilling to gain any significant instruction in the liberal arts. The authors of a recent volume on *Executive Action* stated: "There is no longer such a person as 'the engineer,' but there are a multitude of specialized engineers, many of whose skills are not interchangeable."

Though professors in the liberal arts deplore specialization as a sin of the sciences, many of them live in glass houses. The program for the Ph.D. degree in the liberal arts is often an example of fact-grubbing at its worst. In many colleges the results are reflected in the teaching departments. A college economics department of six teachers includes four specialists who have little knowledge of general economics and still less of history and government. In one university English department of twelve members, eleven declined to teach the undergraduate course in nineteenth-century poetry when the twelfth went on leave for one semester, on the sole grounds that they were not qualified, though all were Doctors of Philosophy and several had taught English in college for twenty years. There are professors of psychology and sociology so vehemently attached to their particular schools of professional thought that they make it difficult for their departments to appoint representatives of any other theory or technique.

In many graduate schools the influence of specialization and fact-worship has made them routine factories for the production of advance-degree holders who are neither good scholars nor good teachers. Their programs and standards are well adapted to encourage the second-rate mind that delights in intellectual drudgery and to repel or dehydrate young men and women with talent, enthusiasm and questing imaginations less easy to regiment and satisfy. The tragedy of graduate-school commencements is that so many emerge from the ceremony, like Adam and Eve from Milton's Paradise, all passion spent. Of the results of this intellectual isolationism Ortega wrote:

"Previously men could be divided into the learned and the ignorant, those more or less the one, and those more or less the other. But your specialist cannot be brought in under either of these two categories. He is not learned, for he is formally ignorant of all that does not enter into his own specialty; but neither is he ignorant, because he is a 'scientist' and 'knows' very well his own tiny portion of the universe. In politics, in art, in social usages, he will adopt the attitudes of primitive, ignorant man; but he will adopt them forcefully and with self-sufficiency, and will not admit of—this is the paradox—specialists in these matters. By specializing him, civilization has made him hermetic and self-satisfied within his limitations; but this very inner feeling of dominance and worth will induce him to wish to predominate outside his speciality. . . . The result is that he will behave in almost all spheres of life as does the unqualified, the mass-man."

Ortega's words are not wholly true. There are specialists who escape the limitations he describes so emphatically. But many are recognizable in Ortega's diatribe, and the description applies accurately to some younger victims of specialization. By breaking into fragments the minds of scholars and the content of knowledge, it attacks the concept of the whole man and of a unified universe; by assigning equal value to each item of knowledge it denies that some are more significant than others, and that to understand man is more important than to understand machines or even atoms. Specialists who concentrate on learning more and more details about limited things are usually unable to translate their learning into any universal meaning, to illumine and fructify the understanding of men and of the infinite. Those with the least vision devote themselves to what is often no more than the infinite elaboration of tremendous trivia, and impart to their students an admiration for the tools of science rather than its goal.

More than scientists themselves realize, they are becoming overwhelmed by the technologies they have created. Their tools, like those of the sorcerer's apprentice, have got out of hand. Applied science is dwarfing fundamental research, and where such research is commercially sponsored it is usually under pressure—indirect at least—to produce results that will be commercially useful to its patrons. Even academic scientists are becoming increasingly the direct or indirect employees of industry or government. The result is too often not an attempt to gain new understanding of the laws of nature but to exploit laws already known, and nothing could be more destructive to the spirit of pure science.

An educational force quite different from specialization has worked in another way toward the bowdlerization of education. The last three decades have seen the rise, distortion and decline of what was called progressive education. At its best it was a corrective to excessive regimentation in education; at its worst a confusion of sentimentality, mediocrity and rationalized indiscipline. In the hands of wise and skilled teachers with high intellectual standards, with a sense of the importance of mental order and personal self-discipline, with plenty of time and money to devote to each pupil, and above all with humor and perspective, progressive education could produce fine results—as what educational system could not? Such teachers and conditions are rare, and the combination existed no more frequently in progressive schools than elsewhere.

Exponents of "conservative" education believed that some areas of life must be regulated in schools as in society, in order to create an atmosphere of respect for order which would encourage the self-discipline essential to human freedom. The theory of progressive education, in its original validity, did not call for the elimination of discipline, but asserted that if all authoritarianism were removed the discipline of the schoolboy would spontaneously develop through the self-regulatory powers it believed inherent in group life and in the social adjustment of the individual. The theory lent itself to easy misuse by the second-rate, the spurious and the intellectually half-baked. In their hands it encouraged the elimination of any previously established standards of content, performance and discipline—and when those are not met the result is hardly education. Inclination guided all. Coming at a time when various forces had weakened social standards and moral authority, progressive education added to the intellectual chaos in the minds of teachers and parents, and aided the trends toward disunity and mediocrity.

For the reasons given and others, American education has not progressed toward the objective defined by William James: "What the colleges . . . should at least try to give us is a general sense of what, under various disguises, superiority has always signified and may still signify. . . . the admiration of the really admirable, the distaste for what is cheap and trashy and impermanent . . . is the better part of what men know as wisdom."

If admiration of the really admirable is the goal of culture, then education must reverse its present trends. It must go back to first principles and define with clarity its goal and the standards by which it proposes to measure quality. The educational institutions of democracy have failed to clarify their ends or to impart precision in thought or in the communication of thought, except in limited reaches of upper scholarship. Precise thought and precise expression are allied; loose thinking leads to vague words, and carelessness of expression corrupts the accuracy of the mind. The nation which excels in the making of precision machinery is weak in the precision of its ideas. The jargons and polysyllables common in several professions and quasi-professions are partly façades to conceal the confusion in second-rate minds. The first step toward a general remedy is greater emphasis on the disciplines of thinking and expression in all schools and all colleges. This can be done. Even so simple a change as a return to the study of grammar in the schools and logic and précis-writing in the colleges might have startling effects.

But reason and accuracy is not all, and education needs another change that will demand time, wisdom, experience and caution. Free society has made no serious comprehensive effort to bring its citizens to an understanding of their own emotions, not as psychiatric cases but as normal men and women. Half the attempts in this field have been abortive from lack of knowledge, skill or patience. Yet present education does little more than to show the intellect how to deal with life piecemeal, without perspective upon oneself and other men. The higher the education the more its emotional aspects have been ignored. Much of the effort of classroom and life is therefore baffling or unsatisfying. Desires men cannot co-ordinate or even understand compete within them and with their feeble reason, or arise to disrupt their pathetic plans of the rational life. They feel the competition of rival emotional claims from within and without themselves, but do not know even how to begin to weave them into a consistent pattern of living and purpose.

The confusions and frustrations that trouble free men cannot be controlled until, without ignoring the life of reason, they understand a little more of the life of the emotions and the claims of the spirit. Private feelings are the background of human hopes and actions. If men did not feel, it would not matter to them what they believed or how they lived. Now that mankind walks the knife edge between freedom and slavery of a new kind, the feelings of individual men and women may seem trivial, but they are the stuff from which everything important in life is made. Education can no longer afford to relegate them to the laboratory, the consulting room and the ill-informed efforts of school and college advisors.

Having clearly defined its values and objectives, education would be in a position to fight for them. It might then be found that society, perhaps with relief, would defer to a united front of educators who knew their minds and would not compromise—who would not shrink from being called the theorists they should be, the idealists they must become, the authoritarians the present chaos demands.

What is needed most of all is a change in the spirit of democratic culture. That can come only after free men reach a common conviction of what they want from life and translate that conviction into consistent daily values. This cannot be done by the forces of education alone, but they can lead more effectively. How they would do so, by what infinite devices and courageous steps, must rest with them. But there are a few obvious goals they could pursue more ardently than at present.

They could distinguish between education as an economic initiation and as a growth of the mind and spirit. They could offer more elevating incentives for study than preparation for a job, for teaching than the holding of a job, for scholarship than the pursuit of the esoteric or the dissection of the entrails of the minor past. They could insist that education be regarded not as a commodity but a privilege and the noblest and most difficult of the arts. They could be more stern in repelling from the curriculum and the campus the irrelevancies and the hypocrisies that flourish there, and thus regain an atmosphere of the primacy and dignity of scholarship. On the strength of these demonstrations, they could then appeal to the mature minds in their communities, not for more money but for more moral support against the pressures of immediacy and mediocrity. This would require that all educational administrators have a sense of the meaning and mission of scholarship; that professors have wider social horizons, and that both have courage and endurance.

Such endeavors would bring them closer to the principles of the great statesmen and educators who preceded them in the development and service of idealistic democracy. They would not, in the long run, fail, for whatever they accomplished would be partial victory. Individual educators might fail; they might suffer for their efforts in a great cause; but they might find out that what they had lost in comfort and security they had gained in self-respect.

13

The People's Choice

For it so falls out
That what we have we prize not to the worth
Whiles we enjoy it, but being lacked and lost,
Why, then we rack the value; then we find
The virtue that possession would not show us
Whiles it was ours.
                    —MUCH ADO ABOUT NOTHING, IV, i.

Civilization has its mysterious regressions, and it seems
to me that we are fated now to be in one of them, and
must recognize this and behave accordingly.
                    —E. M. FORSTER

THE PRECEDING chapters have considered disturbing trends of our democratic society. Though the analysis has not been complete, or all its interpretations beyond debate, two conclusions seem inescapable. Democracy has not elevated the quality of its culture in pace with its material progress. Popular sovereignty can lift itself to higher levels of mind and spirit only by drastic revisions in its current philosophy and in the spirit and performance of its institutions.

If a considerable portion of free society has no firm faith in the values on which it was built or the standards by which those values are measured, then democracy is in real jeopardy. If the present trends continue to their logical ends, the results can be envisaged. Democracy as a political sys-

tem would become an intensely socialized state in which individuals would diminish to insignificance in a uniform
society dominated by the verdicts of transient majorities.
Democracy as a culture would level down to equalitarian
mediocrity, guided by materialism and expediency, and increasingly engendering personal frustrations and group psychoses.

It is a modern cliché that all criticism should be constructive. The critic is expected to offer a concrete remedial
program, thus relieving the reader of formulating one and
giving him something to criticize in his turn. To those who
demand an easy formula for the salvation of democracy the
advice of a Cambridge professor is recommended: select any
five of the Ten Commandments and abide them. It is doubtful that even so drastic a remedy would make democracy
perfect, or that its requirement of fifty-per-cent saintliness
would prove popular. For those who seek solutions more
practical (by which is usually meant less painful) a few
thoughts can be offered, though with no sense of an obligation to provide a happy ending.

The cures for democracy's ills are apparent from their
nature. The removal of confusion begins with a determination to define and face its causes; the cure for mediocrity
with a desire for excellence; the tempering of materialism
with a yearning for values beyond it. Once the needs are
recognized and really wanted, free society should be able to
direct all its institutions toward its own elevation.

The needs are not recognized because democratic man
has neglected to view in perspective the direction in which
he is moving. He has indulged his daily desires with the
assumption that because they were on the whole creditable
they would ultimately bring him to a vaguely conceived
Utopia. He has been dealing with only immediate issues,
hoping that by some beneficent alchemy his piecemeal de-

cisions would be transmuted into a consistent ascent toward ultimate perfection. Americans are acting as though they had long since been permanently set on the right track, and need do no more than stoke the engine and keep moving. As their physical acceleration has carried them rapidly to certain attractive way-stations, they have been diverted from their final destination and have ignored the condition of their rolling-stock.

Democracy's deflection from the ultimate ends of freedom has been too gradual and too happily rationalized to be widely noticed. But each detour has left its sense of direction less acute. Since democratic government, in spite of all its troubles, is obviously preferable to current tyrannies, there has been little incentive to check the compass in democracy's ship of state. Yet events of the century have shown that if a nation becomes lost in immediacy it can be quickly corrupted by propaganda or fall apart through indecision. Hitler and Stalin were able in one generation to pervert the ideals and emotions of societies that had forgotten their goals.

Free men have thought themselves invulnerable to the lures of totalitarianism. But totalitarianism wears more than one cloak, and what dictators can do to society consciously, democracy can do to itself unwittingly. Ideas that corrupt freedom do not politely pause at the threshold of democracy out of delicate respect for its traditions. Free society is thoughtlessly indoctrinating itself with stronger and stronger doses of mental confusions. It will not need direct injections from without if it continues to dilute principle with compromise, to avoid self-analysis by platitudes, to foster the equalitarianism that breeds mediocrity, to tolerate the opportunism that makes human welfare a game of politics and economics a skirmish of group interests, to exalt dubious means at the expense of proper ends. Complacency about democracy could become its greatest menace.

The question raised in the first chapter was whether the increase in popular sovereignty has been a major cause of cultural decline. When two concomitant developments are closely intertwined, it is reasonable to assume a causal relation between them. It does not matter at this stage whether political mass management is the hen and cultural cheapness the egg, or whether the maternity is reversed; the effects are the same. But the assumption of the relationship is supported by much evidence. If the facts presented in earlier chapters have not led the reader to his own conclusion, any final arguments here would be futile. In those areas of life and thought—such as politics, cinema, press, radio, entertainment and mass production—where popular preference has been most compulsive, the symptoms of mediocrity are most apparent.

This is not to ignore other causes of mediocrity. The downward pull of commercial materialism, the decline of moral standards and religious sanctions, the corruption of education and the spiritual destructions and tensions of war and cold war have all played their part. How adverse would have been their effects had they not been accompanied by mass sovereignty can be no more than a speculation. Certainly popular sovereignty accepted them and disseminated them.

One can do no more than guess at the extent to which war and the threat of war atrophies cultural ideals. The morale of the free world had by no means recovered from the corrosions of the first world war when the second war began. Future centuries will bear the psychic scars of this century's hatreds and destructions, even if they go no further. But democracy's ills cannot all be laid to war, for some of the forces that created those ills were in operation before Sarajevo and have augmented since Nagasaki. The infections of democracy began within itself, and military events only speeded and strengthened their corruption.

Government by the people was for centuries an ideal. It has not been proved an empty one, but events have demonstrated that the extension of popular sovereignty does not automatically elevate humanity. Indeed, it has made the task of civilization more complicated, for to call the masses to power is to dilute existing culture and to risk the capacity of large numbers of ordinary men to advance a civilization which only exceptional men were able to create. If the dominant majority continues to be confused in its values, trivial in its interests, vulgar in its tastes and ignoble in its aims, then popular sovereignty will be no road to elevation. Instead of being the seed-bed of man's highest potentialities, freedom will become merely the hard-packed playground of shallow and self-seeking materialism.

Free men need not conclude from their somewhat disillusioning experience that popular rule inevitably brings mediocrity. The cure lies in their own hands, and they are not bankrupt of energy or ideals. But to avoid political decay they must revise their present interpretation of the phrase "government by the people." More government by the people does not invariably bring more freedom to the people or ensure wiser statesmanship. All forms of government can be beneficent or tyrannical, moderate or excessive, and democracy is no exception. The present interpretations of democracy could lead to tyranny—by the majority.

Free society can eliminate that danger only if it becomes willing to rank its men and its ideas according to their quality and to the excellence of their contribution to spiritual as well as mundane welfare. It must go further and agree with both Jefferson and Hamilton that the voice of the people serves its purpose best when its tones are restrained and its accent cultivated. To many Americans the idea of any alteration in full political and cultural dominance by the people will seem at variance with the philosophy of Lincoln when he spoke of "government by the people." But when Lincoln used that phrase he associated it with two other phrases, and must have thought the three inseparable. He wanted government not only by the people but of the people and for the people. "By the people" means residual power in the people; "of the people" that even free men must yield the active reins of government to some agents other than themselves *en masse;* and government "for the people" implied that, though the administration of the government must be in their behalf, it could not be subject to their detailed direction.

It is still possible—though it will be very difficult—for American society to develop an aristocracy of talents and virtue. This does not mean the creation of a fixed, pampered group of oligarchs or plutocrats, but an ordered series of flexible levels throughout society. To create it, a change would be required in the attitudes of most Americans. The thought of any aristocracy or elite, no matter how democratic its methods of recruitment, is unpalatable to them. It will remain unpalatable, and hence impossible, until free society ardently desires to elevate its ways.

This means that society would have to mature its values. It could do so only by enlisting all the agencies of culture to drive in conscious unity toward that end. Education would have to revise its policies as well as its curriculum to bring the core of humane learning into the minds of all those it instructs. The churches would have to find interpretations of their spiritual ideals which, without compromising their quality, would seem valid and important to superior and average minds alike. Those who make goods would have to find ways to bring into their systems a premium on human excellence as well as technical or administrative efficiency;

those who sell goods, to find appeals that do not glorify the acquisition of motor cars and hi-fi sets as the highest end of man. Those who provide communication and entertainment in all their forms would have to take far more seriously their responsibility to elevate the tastes of society.

No nation has ever attempted such a task on so large a scale, or under a social system dominated by those who are to be the subjects of their own reform. Would tens of millions of Americans willingly substitute rigorous intellectual discipline for loose thinking and magic formulae? Would they willingly put the pains and austerities of spiritual self-searching before current comfort and bodily security? Would they willingly rid themselves of the primitive envies and mistaken political ideas that have led them to oppose superiority in all but the most adolescent forms? Is free society too satisfied with itself as it is; has it accepted the rationalization that by raising its material level ever higher it will surely find the cultural and ethical levels automatically rising; does it believe that it can muddle through to the good life without giving and using its best?

Society's advance depends upon its emphatic recognition of the need for placing its highest value on the individual. This is the unit for which it exists and upon which its future in freedom rests. Civilization is the product, not primarily of laws or social organization, but of individual men and women—their capacities, ideals and efforts. Society can never possess or represent all the depth and promise of the human entity.

Democracy was rooted in a respect for man as a human personality, and every step along the path to social freedom has been through its development and protection. Democracy did not rest its case, and cannot now rest its case, on man merely as a biological sport, an economic unit, a psychological complex or a cell in the social organism. If it did, all that freedom would mean would be aimless and acquisitive relativity within the tight bounds of an all-powerful state. That is why fascists and communists who seek to undermine democracy belittle and violate the dignity and religion of the individual man. They know that if they can destroy his primacy they have destroyed democracy. It was the mutual conviction of Christianity and democracy that every man contains the spark of the divine which made them allies: that was a truth that seemed to Jefferson self-evident.

To protect and utilize this truth, democracy must guard against contrary theories drawn from mechanics, commerce, science or false liberalism. The more highly organized society becomes, the greater its difficulty in protecting its individuals against itself. When the state overgrazes the human pasture it makes a spiritual desert. When the welfare of a vague entity called society is placed before the importance of the individual, human personality ceases to be sacred. Democracy loses the support of religion, to whom the soul of each separate man is the primary concern.

The tests of a good society are its riches in human personalities and the chances it gives them for self-development. If democracy fails those tests it abandons its own foundations. The French revolutionaries attempted to establish the rights of man on reason alone, and planted the seeds of their own failure. They regarded the rights of the individual as derived from his utility to the state, and thus subordinated the man to the mass. So does socialism, so does communism, so does fascism. The only rights of the free citizen then become whatever the majority, or the Leader, sees fit to allow him. When this happens, free government has swung the full circle, and delivered the rights of man back to their original enemy—arbitrary power in any form which ignores the spark of Zeus or Jehovah in every man.

Democracy must therefore take no liberties with a man's personal liberty. Yet in modern democratic society the individual's personal privacy is attacked by mass living, his personal contemplation by mass activity, his personal self-realization by mass conformity. The individual will continue at odds with the mass until society establishes absolute values more affirmative than pragmatism and incentives more elevating than the pursuit of power and security. The backbone of a body politic is clear ethical values. Athenian liberty died, according to Lord Acton, because its age possessed no fixed standards of right and wrong. History bequeathed us some standards—by no means perfect ones but the best the human experience had evolved. Modern free men can depend upon them as a working code, for the ethical verdicts of the centuries have rarely been reversed. Americans cannot afford to let the whir of machinery or the blare of salesmen and entertainers drown out the voices of earlier wisdom or the music of the spheres.

Most confused liberals oppose absolute values on the grounds that they are authoritarian and hence tend toward fascism. This is a double fallacy. All authority is not fascistic and all standards are not authoritarian. The society whose members freely agree upon and maintain ethical absolutes is the society least vulnerable to fascism. The crucial point is whether the absolutes are imposed from without or are voluntarily observed. Personal absolutes personally maintained are the essence of democracy and the antithesis of dictatorship. Freedom is itself one of the absolutes, a standard by which men can measure their lives, and only men who can maintain firm values can maintain freedom. In their absence, the state assumes the moral role, and gains in authority until its rule becomes an end in itself, and rectitude becomes whatever the state says it is.

We are having a preview of the state as the only definer of virtue in some of its investigations of nonconformist individuals. The state, or its committees, can only assume such a role when society is caught without common value convictions and standards of right procedure. Marxism has its appeal to men with value vacuums because it lets them hide their uncertainties behind the fatalism of economic determinism. Communism goes further, and relieves men of every decision and every standard by the dictum that there is only one absolute virtue—the party. There can be no morality, and hence no freedom, unless men possess the courage and the will to make their own decisions.

If these were the only factors that determine democracy, its future would be gloomy indeed. There are others that give grounds for hope, if not for optimism. Man's dissatisfaction with himself and his way of life has always been the leaven of history. There are signs, still rare and fragile, that that leaven is at work in America. Amid the clatter of machine and the chatter of conformity one hears undertones of protest against the emptiness and uniformity of our high-powered life. Men are finding that with all their outward liberties and prosperity their spirits are confined and unfed, and that they cannot be more free than the range of their own mental vision. They are beginning to wonder whether the reason why science and psychology have failed to find a soul in man is because they do not know where or how to look for it. An increasing number of intransigents are not willing to continue to excuse modern civilization with the familiar phrase that this is an age of transition; they are demanding that it become an age creative of men and beauty as well as of physical power. They suspect that the real message of relativity is that there can be fixity wherever men choose to establish it. They hope that the essence of liberty may prove to be freedom to renounce the commonplace. Such voices may increase in number and volume.

One such voice is that of a learned judge who recently summarized his dream of what the American way of life should sometime be. It would be a life in which speed and change would no longer infatuate society. The individual would not be an anonymous atom wandering after a kind of mechanical progress the very pursuit of which was irritating. The harsh domination of the machine would be mellowed and warmed by personal associations and rewards derived from mutual consideration among all men. Society would develop humane traditions to check and chasten those who tried to make it conform to their personal pattern. Men of great promise would be encouraged to develop above general conformity, and they would thus temper the volatile ecstasies and emotional conclusions that sweep over the undigested thinking of popular society.

The only real hope for the elevation of democracy lies in the sincerity and spread of reactions such as these. The promise of a cultural renascence lies not in the quantitative increase of cultural activity; not in the turning of men outward to meet and adjust to the latest mores of society, but in inward searching by many individuals to find their personal means of self-realization. In their efforts to escape from the compulsions and diversions of mass life, the first attempts of some of us are immature or illusory, but the desire and the effort give promise.

It is especially impressive that so many young people, who a few years ago seemed superficial in their aims and hedonistic in their standards, have begun to move consciously toward simplicity and self-deepening. They are discovering what they can do with their own minds and their own hands. The results, even if crude, prove more satisfying to them than what they can buy. From such beginnings might come a

nation-wide recrudescence of pleasure in the personally created, the unique, the non-commercial.

Reflection and introspection are not the habits of most
Americans, but if millions of them should begin to reflect
about their own lives, about what they really want from
them and what they must deny themselves to get it, the com-
plexion of American society would change rapidly. It would
change for the better, but it would still be relatively shallow.
The crisis of the times is moral, and the only hope for democracy depends upon whether or not it can revitalize itself
as a moral force, at home as well as abroad. The key to a
better world is the capacity to imagine it, plus the strength
to attempt it. That strength must be moral strength.

We must regain our perspective of ourselves. Even Americans are only a part of the stream of human history and we
delude ourselves if we try to ignore it. Only when a people
begins to see its own thoughts and emotions as part of the
long ascent of humanity does it start to mature. We creators
of the atomic age need not feel that to identify ourselves with
earlier men who knew not mass destruction belittles our
stature or makes us hapless victims of predestination. We are
both makers of new progress and agents of past progress, and
to share in humanity's growth may be our only immortality.

Men who urge a deepening of tradition and faith are not,
in spite of reports to the contrary, defying the progress of
modern science. Science and the spirit are not in opposition
but complementary. Because science is neutral regarding
humane values, the scope of its service to mankind is limited. It cannot civilize the emotions or ameliorate materialism. It cannot uplift the heart or guide the spirit. This is the
business of the older arts, and free society will not realize
its cultural promise until it stops regarding philosophy, religion, letters and the arts as decorative but secondary, to
be acquired by commercial transaction as adornments for

economic man. Society cheats itself when it makes art smart, literature a fashion, education a ready-made suit, philosophy a game of chess and religion the last refuge of the defeated. When thought or creation must be molded to what is chic, they lose their integrity and society loses its standard for evaluating them. Emotional sincerity must be the first criterion in judging art and thought, rejecting all pretense, patronage and desire to conform.

After all the virtues and weaknesses of democracy have been listed and trial balances for its future struck, one immeasurable consideration remains. In the last analysis the future of democracy depends upon whether men really understand it and believe in it. To do so, they must believe in the innate virtue of free men, and their capacity to gain wisdom. Americans have preserved that belief, though often their reasons for their faith are shallow and their expression of it only thoughtless repetition. But even in that weakened form it is still the nation's greatest strength. It can move mountains that will not yield to reason, diplomacy or force; it can save democracy from cynicism and decay. But only on conditions, and they are hard ones.

The first condition is that the American idea of democracy must grow up from a vestigial tradition to a personal conviction, from a conversational commonplace to a social dynamic. We must refresh ourselves at the springs of our own freedom. We must remember that the roots of good government and good society are moral and spiritual roots. Belief in the essential wisdom and good will of men, belief in freedom, must be concrete and self-renewing. It becomes valid and sentient only when he who professes it bases his confidence not on an abstract sea of unknown and inchoate faces, but on the familiar features of actual men and women in whose personal qualities he has come to believe. He cannot trust democratic society unless he can trust its home personifications—the local garage man, the butcher, the school teacher, the salesman, the housewife next door. Only if they seem to him to justify faith in democracy can democracy be justified.

Do these familiar and fallible figures, daily revealing good will and prejudice, vision and blindness, generosity and selfishness, fortify hope in free society? Not if our belief must be based solely on the evidence of things seen. It is what some individual men and women are, and what all could become, that makes confidence in the voice of the people possible. Faith in them, like all faiths, must be based on the evidence of things unseen, on the potential ethos of free society's capacity to lift its average citizens from what they are to what they can be. Democracy is faith in the human potential.

Economic progress, scientific mastery, alert opportunism, education—even security, health and good will—cannot elevate men to wisdom and vision. Something must happen to free men which will raise their spirits to exhilarating missions of self-discovery. True democracy is a self-dedicated adventure of the spirit. When modern men rouse themselves to go on that adventure, they will cease to be cautious pensioners of democracy; they will move with confidence and zest toward the high realities of a finer freedom. Then the sovereign voice of the people will no longer be lifted in discordant confusion, but uplifted in harmony to the measure of their mutual thought.

Freedom cannot make men great, but men can make freedom great. What does America want from freedom? That is the people's choice.